Izabela Luiza Jahn

Stay away from idiots

Imprint

Bibliographic information of the German National Library: The German National Library lists this publication in the German National Bibliography; detailed bibliographic data are available on the Internet at http://dnb.dnb.de.
© 2019 Izabela Luiza Jahn (German Edition)
Cover photo: Izabela Luiza Jahn
© 2022 Izabela Luiza Jahn (English Edition)

Production and publishing house: BoD - Books on Demand, Norderstedt

Bibliografische Information der Deutschen Nationalbibliothek: Die Deutsche Nationalbibliothek verzeichnet diese Publikation in der Deutschen Nationalbibliografie; detaillierte bibliografische Daten sind im Internet über http://dnb.dnb.de abrufbar.
© 2022 Izabela Luiza Jahn
Umschlagfoto: Izabela Luiza Jahn
Übersetzung ins Englische: deepl.com & Izabela Luiza Jahn

Herstellung und Verlag: BoD – Books on Demand, Norderstedt
ISBN: 9783755716754

For Anthony de Mello, the man who first lit a light in the darkness of my conditioning

TABLE OF CONTENTS

III. HAPPY RELATIONSHIPS

PROLOGUE: PSYCHO-LOGICAL

For a better understanding of this book: it all started with a small blog text, and over time it became more and more. This may explain the structure of the individual chapters and the fact that everything is free-form, and may also refer to changes of year.

The aim of the blog, which no longer exists, was to briefly and succinctly present the findings of new, as well as tried and tested, psychological books and guidebooks in terms of their practical benefits, and to show how a diametrically different life can be led through certain conscious decisions and targeted changes. Psychology has fascinated me for some time, because without a certain level of self-knowledge that it can provide, everything is indeed nothing. We live mechanically, not knowing what is happening to us. Every now and then we make a few rationalizing thoughts that justify our actions in retrospect and that are supposed to confirm us. It just does not change anything. Just avoid concern. But maybe this is exactly what we need to really live our own free and self-determined life?

The blog started like this with the question back then:

"There is no point in sitting in a corner and meditating on oneself. [...] I exist only in relation to people, things and ideas, and by examining my relation to external things and people as well as to internal things, I begin to understand myself. Any other form of understanding is only an abstraction [...] I am not an abstract being." Jiddu Krishnamurti[1]

Have you ever noticed that the very people who dislike psychology and psychologists would probably benefit the most from a consultation? The putting down, joking and verbalizing serves to discredit psychology, to play down problems and ultimately to distract and divert attention from oneself. I think that every person knows deep inside that there is something wrong with him. Only he does not want to see it. He doesn't want to look at any price to avoid pain. He does not want to see himself in all his smallness and limitedness. He still wants to believe that he is really great (or really bad) and that the others are to blame/bad/whatever, but not better. So that he doesn't have to give that up, he has been given the gift of repression. And if that's not enough - there's distraction, as we've seen. Some hard drugs, if needed. Alcohol. Whatever. Oh yes - and hubris. Especially the latter has the ability to make others unhappy. And other people also become unhappy by believing that "if only...". Hope dies at last, but people are said to have died before it...

How can I tell that I am a candidate? It's simple: are you happy? Or are you unhappy, even though you are trying hard to live a good life? Are you living your life? Or are you panting after some ideal image? How are your relationships? With your parents, friends, at work? What about your most intimate relationship? Is there any intimacy at all in your marriage or partnership? Or is it hell on earth? Do you also sing the "if only" song? How is your relationship with yourself? Are you your best friend? If not, wouldn't it be nice to change that? If you change, then the whole world changes... just understand why mankind always tries it the other way around ;)

I. UNHAPPY RELATIONSHIPS

CHAPTER 1

SHOW ME YOUR RELATIONSHIP AND I'LL TELL YOU WHO YOU ARE

It shows itself best and most clearly in the most intimate, so I'm talking here about the couple relationship (could also be the one with parents or other very important people for you, and usually these relationships are also affected, although not so extremely, if there are problems in the closest relationship). So, how is it, your relationship? Is it happy? (If so, don't read the nonsense here and do something nice for yourself or with your partner). If "happy relationship" is a surreal idea for you, and for you it is just a matter of bare survival every day between quarrels, humiliation, insults, active and passive aggression, disrespect, threats and indifference, then read on.

Especially when your partner can drive you to despair or to white heat through extremely inaudible actions. If you thereby become a howling, nagging, hysterical monster, and ultimately only whimpering for affection, devoid of any emotional control, and all that against your better judgment. When you no longer feel like yourself because you are so tempted to conform, and to please your partner. To get at least a crumb of his attention or approval. If you have the feeling of loneliness, restlessness, guilt, or fear of loss, of frustration and helplessness in your relationship, then I have two messages for you.

First the good: the fact that another person can touch you deeply is evidence that you are capable of love and commitment. This is good for you. (Right now, though, it probably doesn't feel that way because you're trying in the wrong place).
The bad: Your problem is you're still there. Please let that sink in: Your problem is that you still remain in this relationship on these terms, or at all. That is your part of the problem. With the genesis of the problem, and with the question, how you can get YOUR life back (or

get to know yourself at all?) I want to deal in the further course. For today I would like to conclude with a quote, which in my opinion expresses the essence of love as a gift:

"[Love] is like a fragrant flower. You can perceive its fragrance or pass by it. This flower is there for everyone, and especially for the one who takes the time to breathe in its fragrance intimately and look at it with delight."[2]

Three guesses who this is from ;) But the essential idea is: you don't need to earn love. All you need is someone who is capable of responding to the love you have to give.

CHAPTER 2

ASKING THE RIGHT QUESTIONS

If your friends make you understand that you only talk about your partner, then it's probably time for you to take your life back. And to do this with the same energy with which you have been circling around your partner until now. The entire "why" and "wherefore" and "how can he do this to me" didn't really do anything - did it? Why don't you use the energy you have spent on such questions to ask yourself what YOU need to be well? To ask yourself what makes you happy.

I know that this is not easy, and that you would like to understand the why and wherefore on the one hand, but on the other hand you are just as unlikely to accept it when this question keeps catching up with you. It's understandable, you love someone and they keep acting impossible. For you it is always a slap in the face, a shock. Even though you know from experience, for example, that your partner is always disrespectful to you, or otherwise hurtful, it hits you every time anew with maximum harshness. Understandable, but note that you are caught up by it again and again, because you do not want to admit this trait of your partner. If you would accept this trait and not deny it anymore, it would be easier for you to distance yourself from it. And don't misunderstand me; I'm not talking here about "putting up with him better", but about no longer letting him beat you down, and thus being able to meet your partner differently.

Furthermore, the desire to understand and fathom why your partner behaves the way he does can also be paralyzing for YOU - and here it is quite irrelevant whether you feel too much "understanding", or even more confusion by thinking too long. If you are more concerned with your partner's problems than he is, something is wrong. It is an adult human being who should stand up for his problems (regardless of what was, and with help if necessary - but not YOURS - you are not a therapist, are you?). So ask yourself: how much does my partner's behavior absorb me?

CHAPTER 3

"WHY ME?"

I realize that a "this is your partner's problem, and you are not his/her therapist" is not sufficient as an explanation, especially since, for one thing, you must have spent a lot of time asking "why", feeling guilty for the problems in the relationship, or being blamed for your partner's misbehavior by him/her.... Or, and I think this is why the "why" keeps us going for so long, because you hope that if you somehow understand it all, you can change something about it, and finally have the relationship you hope and desire.

So let's start there: you have to understand that you can't change anything. Not the way you are trying to do it now. You have an attachment disordered, either fearful-avoidant or indifferent-avoidant partner, a narcissistic or otherwise toxic person with whom you are trying to have a relationship. Trying is a good description, because the above mentioned people are not able and not willing to have a relationship, even if they like to declare it differently. Sometimes. Occasionally. When it suits them or the mood is good. Because unfortunately these people are deeply disturbed in their ability to commit, and here wanting does not necessarily mean being able. What I want to say - if you want to understand why your partner behaves the way he/she does: he/she is disturbed in his/her bonding ability and he/she was already disturbed before you. He/she had exactly the same problems then. It has nothing to do with you. That is what you have to understand.

It just doesn't feel that way.... That's because you pay for trying to have a relationship with an attachment disordered person with loss of control. The fact is, this gives the attachment avoider power over the relationship, which is thus not at eye level. He is the sole ruler of closeness and distance; he determines the relationship and is uncompromising. This is a very perfidious mechanism of such relationships, which I will discuss in more detail.

But this mechanism can work only because:

- Your partner denies you something you really want. Since you actually want a relationship with your partner, you are at a disadvantage.

- You put the desire to keep this relationship going or finally get it going above your own well-being.

That's why you.

CHAPTER 4

THE SCHEME: "MY WAY OR HIGHWAY".

You never thought you'd put up with something like that, did you? Ever thought about taking the blackmailing threat "then look for someone else, if you don't like it, that's it" seriously? To say "Thanks, you're right; I've wasted enough time here. I deserve a person who really wants to be in a relationship with me. Who is interested in me, and for whom this is not an imposition. Who is capable of real closeness, and for whom being in the same room isn't already a problem." No? Too bad...

The fact is that the attachment disordered person tells you that without batting an eye is because he can say it. He really doesn't care (and that's why you can't sit it out or turn the tables - the attachment disordered person always wins, if you can even talk about winning here). He shifts the responsibility to you; you can adapt, or leave it alone. Because what he doesn't want at any price in the world is to have a closer look on himself. In this price you are included. And that is hard to accept. Aptly, Stefanie Stahl writes that "[...] a person without attachment anxiety usually cannot even imagine how little it takes to get too close to an attachment phobe. Often, just being present is enough. Or just calling. The problem is, you can't not get too close to the commitment phobe. No matter how reserved you act, somehow you always get too close to him if you want to have a relationship with him. "[3]

Only, in the beginning it looked totally different? Didn't it? Then your partner didn't feel "crushed" by your "expectations", "restricted in his/her space" by a "leech" (which you have become now), "annoyed" by your "bitching" and your "seeing problems where there are none".

If it's any consolation: that you should be terrible right now has nothing to do with you. You are in phase two of the typical relationship progression with a disturbed person. Now that he has you, he can't and won't put up with you, because you might want to have a normal happy relationship. But that's exactly what your partner can't do. Have you ever wondered why he becomes so hurtful or abusive, all of a sudden for no apparent reason, especially when things seem to be going well at the moment? There are many perverse reasons for this, the main one being this: Your partner doesn't believe this relationship is able to be going well. "Consciously or unconsciously [he] expects it to fail. So that they are not so helplessly at the mercy of this catastrophe [for their low self-esteem], [partners who are incapable of bonding] actively ensure (keyword: control) that they bring it about themselves. It is the well-known phenomenon of the "self-fulfilling prophecy" that can be observed here. They use biting remarks, venomous comments, and outright arguments to regulate the closeness that feels too threatening to them. By doing this, they distance the partner, who reacts sadly, disappointedly, and/or angrily, as the case may be. With this tactic, they repeatedly strain the relationship and put it to the test. Depending on the partner's capacity for suffering, this can lead to continuous power struggles and pointless arguments or even to the end of the relationship. Either way, the attachment disordered person proves to himself what he already knew anyway: relationships don't work out."[4] I want to emphasize again, actually your partner doesn't think *relationship* goes well *at all*, and that has nothing to do with you as a person. However, phase one, where you were great and desired had nothing to do with you either. You are the object on which all this takes place. And replaceable, that is then phase three, when it becomes too exhausting with you, or you have finally left. If necessary, phase one to two will be repeated with you again in phase three, if you make the mistake of returning.

I know it's not nice to hear. But the truth is not always pleasant. However, only through the truth do you gain the freedom to make your decisions.

Next time I will write about when it's better to leave. And about what you should take to heart (keyword loss of control) if you don't. After all, you are only human ;)

CHAPTER 5

WHEN IT IS BETTER TO GO

If you ask me: better yesterday than tomorrow. The longer the condition lasts like this, the more often your partner promised changes and didn't keep them, or the clearer he/she told you that he/she doesn't care - honestly, we have only a short flash as a life span - go.

Why this is difficult: think about the 3 phases of the relationship. In the beginning, in the phase of being in love, you have been implanted with a relationship illusion that has never been fulfilled, but has turned into its opposite. There has never been a feeling of being securely bound. How could there be? But unfortunately, "[the] need to have control over one's life and to feel a certain security is an existential, basic psychological need. This existential need couples to the need for attachment, which is equally existential. Every person who enters into a love relationship and thus fulfills his or her need for attachment desires a certain degree of security and the feeling that he or she can rely on the partner. Conversely, not having security is enormously frightening. Fatally, however, the loss of control, that is, the fear of losing the other person, fuels passion enormously. So instead of relaxing, according to the motto "if he/she doesn't want to, then he/she doesn't! "the insecurity triggers exactly the opposite impulse in most partners: namely to want him/her now more than ever. [I would rather say: to want the promised relationship to finally start, because your partner has aroused a lot of expectations in you, and behaves completely contradictory and leaves you emotionally starved after he/she promised you a feast]. Behind this is the deeply human need to (re)gain control. "[5] And you know how stupid your behavior is; only you still can't let it go. That's loss of control: caring about a person even though they are harming you. It's an ego thing, after all, you're great, and your partner used to see it that way too, and promised you everything imaginable... if only you go back there, and finally live that....

Please remember the 3 phases, it was not real. Just a projection on you. Do not insist on it. Don't make yourself miserable. Do like yourself for real. Again. Because the loss of control means that you are no longer yourself. Stop tying your well-being and especially your self-worth to this person. It's never going to be enough. It's a black hole. For God's sake, do NOT ask "what am I doing wrong?". At most, you're still there, nothing else. Why don't you focus on your happiness for a change...?

How to do it (with or without a partner) soon. Take care of yourself.

CHAPTER 6

PRACTICALLY, THE PROCEDURE - WHETHER YOU WANT TO SEPARATE OR NOT - IS THE SAME IN BOTH CASES:

In order for anything to truly change, you have to accept the end of your relationship.

Otherwise, you will just keep spinning as before, and the behavior patterns leading to loss of control will remain. What these are, and how you can recognize them, I think is best explained by a small list of questions from Bärbel Wardetzki's book "Eitle Liebe"[6] , which aims to find out whether you are in the so-called "expanded self" of another person. Her book deals with narcissism, however I find that the behavioral patterns described in it can be found in all relationships however dysfunctional and toxic. So here are the questions, for one:

"How can you tell that you are in someone else's "expanded self"?

- Do you feel inferior, small, not good enough, void in contact?
- Or, on the contrary, do you feel special and inappropriately valorized? [This happens naturally at the beginning of the relationship, I think the English expression is Love Bombing]
- Do you experience her or him as ideal and superior?
- Do you not dare to act spontaneously?
- Do you control your impulses and behavior?
- Do you not dare to tell the other person honestly how you are and what you need?
- Do you always have an eye on what your counterpart might like?
- Do you behave and feel rather awkward and ungrown? Maybe like you know it from your childhood?
- Are you experiencing anxiety, panic, feelings of abandonment, depression, or physical states that are not appropriate for the situation and seem excessive to yourself?
- Nevertheless, can you not stop these states in contact with the other person?
- Do you resort to addictive substances to calm yourself, distract yourself from your feelings, or to cope with the situation?
- Do you see yourself through the other person's eyes and try to match the other person's image?
- Are you fooling yourself and the other person?
- Are you not at all the person you pretend to be, just to please or to win over your counterpart?
- Do you deny everything you don't want to see in the other person?
- Do you first even recognize and feel the other person's rejection and devaluations when you are alone?
- In contact with the other person, do you not see a way to distance yourself from his/hers influence?
- Do you behave differently than usual?
- Do you put a lot of effort into the contact? "[7]

If you can answer some things in the affirmative, you may be forced to ask how this could have happened. Here's what happened:

"How can you tell that the other person is creating an "expanded self" with you?

- The other person showes their best behavior. [at the beginning]
- She/ he expects to be idealized by you in return.
- Your counterpart defines how you should be, mostly non-verbally.
- Your counterpart expects you to meet this definition and will react negatively if you do not.
- If you behave differently than your counterpart expects, he/she will try to manipulate or devalue you.
- Or it even comes to manifest disputes such as: loud arguments, accusations, reproaches, strong tensions and, in the worst case, relationship breakdown.
- You will be rewarded if you are willing to reflect [your partner's idealized self-image back to them.] [...]
- Or you can achieve it by being the way your counterpart wants you to be and thereby deriving benefit from you [...].
- Your counterpart makes you feel that power is important to him/her, and he/she is not afraid to "subdue" you.[8]

If you let the questions sink in, and consider what kind of non-relationship (that's more what I would call it) underlies them, I hope you won't find it so hard to put up with the end of it. Now comes the essential question:

How do I get out of it?

- Accept the end of your relationship, otherwise you will remain susceptible to blackmail and fall back into these behavior patterns again and again for fear of confronting your partner and thus losing them. You need to change the frame of reference. Until now, it was the preservation of the relationship. Now it should be your well-being.

- Trusting in your partner's love and that he has only your best interests at heart, you have granted your partner power and influence over you. Disempower him, because empowerments can be withdrawn, and should be, if your counterpart obviously does not deserve them and uses them against you. I would like to show here in all clarity, you are not powerless, because it is YOUR decision whether you grant your partner influence over you or not. Only those who are free can choose.

- If you need someone else's opinion about you, find people who appreciate you and can give you an honest but loving opinion about yourself. Stop taking neither criticism nor compliments (yes, even those, emotional yo-yo effect) from your partner at face value. I once saw a fabulous cartoon about this, where a master pours out a regular "educational" torrent of words about his dog. The speech bubble above the dog's head read, "Blah, blah Rex, blah Rex". Be a little like Rex. I know it's radical, but it's helpful if you start on the path back to yourself, if you first emotionally distance yourself from your partner, and become completely independent of his influence and opinion. Otherwise, your partner can easily send you on an emotional roller coaster with a few words, or a snide look, and you do a few more loops in the relationship in your old behaviors.

- This also includes: don't be there more often. Do what you enjoy all by yourself. Preferably outdoors, with other people. Discover forgotten or new hobbies, revive your favorite sport of your youth, or finally take that yoga class. Anything that does you good, gets you moving, puts you in touch with other people, and makes you feel alive and free and exuberant again is exactly what you need right now. And not someone who tries to tell you for the hundred thousandth time how bad and inadequate you are.

- Draw your personal boundaries clearly! Be clear about what you will accept and what you will not. Clearly show the consequences. Be careful not to make empty threats. Then your partner will learn: "Blah,

blah, blah, Rex." I will show you exactly how to do this in specific situations.

Because, if you succeed in finding yourself again, and to make yourself independent from your partner in a healthy way, it can be that just him, who still wanted to remain so gladly unmolested by you, nevertheless lacks your availability, which was available for him so far at any time, and he, to express his displeasure, starts to behave worse than ever...

CHAPTER 7

UNLEARNING LEARNED HELPLESSNESS

That is what needs to be done now. In the previous chapters I have shown some behavioral patterns and cycles that in sum make you feel frustrated, angry, helpless and almost disoriented in a relationship with a toxic person, so that you actually started doubting your sanity. This is not by chance, because your partner has given everything to make you believe that "there is no problem, everyone would react like that if provoked by you like that", "lighten up, I didn't mean it" (when he insulted you), or "you don't just look for problems, you downright make some." And you?

You have, at first perhaps out of false indulgence taken it to you: "yes it was hurtful, but he/she didn't mean it that way", "I shouldn't have provoked him/her like that". You did it out of false feelings of guilt, or to avoid further trouble "I'd rather not say anything, it will only get worse". You have gone along with the dance, hoping to bring peace and harmony back into your relationship. The result is that you are now dancing to the tune of your partner until you completely give up on yourself, rewarding him for his misbehavior, because he gets what he wants and can do anything he wants. There are no consequences for him. Furthermore, by taking the blame, not asking for things in the first place and putting your own needs behind or having given up long ago (peace at any price, right?) you are just reinforcing your partner in the rightness of his actions. And moreover: your partner is far away from having to admit that he/she is the problem. These are, in fact, people who shirk responsibility for their actions and the effects they have on others, and have made "never apologize" their motto in life. That's only cool on NAVY CIS. Not otherwise.

So think: how do you reward your partner's bad behavior? How do you help your partner not to feel problems and negative consequences that he/she should feel because of his/her behavior?

Wondering how to do that? Here is an example from Townsend's book in my translation. It's about a father - daughter relationship: "When your father criticizes you for no reason, you try to appease him. If he has behaved cruelly, you call him and apologize for provoking him. If he has a good day, you hope that he will change, while he simply recovers and gathers strength to commit new badness the day after tomorrow. That's why when he explodes again; it catches you completely off guard. Like everyone, you avoid direct confrontation with him, so he never gets an honest opinion about his behavior. You don't demand that he undergo therapy because it might enrage him. [...] If your siblings are mad at him, you try to mediate so he doesn't get upset."[9] Etc., etc.

You may not be able to make your partner change. But you can let go of all these behaviors described above so that this pathological dance will automatically stop. I once heard the beautiful saying, "Life itself points out the most applicable consequences." Let it happen, don't keep them away from your partner. Take back control of your own life by clearly setting your own boundaries and defining what behavior you will and will not accept. What alternatives you will accept and what the consequences will be if your partner doesn't stop with their behavior. We will now look at how to do this in individual situations.

CHAPTER 8

I HAVE TRIED "EVERYTHING" AND "NOTHING" HAS HELPED

If you found yourself in the last chapter, I would rather say "no, not quite". For one thing, because you have established many behaviors that disadvantage you, for example, to appease your partner, which only makes him feel more in the right, and reinforces his negative and toxic behaviors when he wants to achieve something. In addition, the ever-faster spinning cycle, falsely reinforces you in the mindset that you can't change anything, and only have to react somehow to prevent the "worst" from happening. If, nevertheless, a justified doubt arises in your mind, the stress that the permanent uncertainty and the feeling of having absolutely lost control permanently creates in you will wear you down so much that you will not be able to think clearly.

The latter can actually be explained by the fact that a person whose basic needs for security, recognition, fulfillment (self-actualization) and control (in the sense of effective design of life) are not met, lives in a state of permanent tension and threat, which in the long run can even lead to physical and emotional problems. (See W. Robert Nay)[10] As we have seen in the first chapters, these are exactly the things that a toxic or otherwise attachment-disordered partner denies us!!! According to Dr. Nay, "Such unfortunate feelings as restlessness, guilt, anger, and fear are a direct effect of having had one of your basic needs negated in some way. Such painful sensations have their purpose. They signal to us that we are at risk of being hurt and that someone or something is threatening the fulfillment of our basic needs."[11] Unfortunately, the more emotional and hurt we become, "the more we run the risk of our partner's behavior turning us into someone we don't want to be and revealing our bad nature in a frightening way. [...] The point is that we feel a need: for warmth, acceptance or love, and expect this from the difficult person. When we don't receive these things, we no longer react in an adult way, but in a desperate and very emotional way."[12] Essentially, this happens because people under tremendous stress fall back on early childhood behavior patterns (called regress, well known in psychology, it probably happens because these are "more firmly" established, and automatically retrieved. Unfortunately, it contributes to the magnification of the problem, especially if you were not lucky enough to have had a happy childhood). "As a rule, this is very ineffective. The toxic person thinks to himself, 'Here you go. I'm not the problem; It is the loopy, frothing woman."[13] And you believe that too, and question yourself. That makes you feel even more insecure, and adds to the emotional chaos that shapes and defines your life with a toxic partner. That's why I was just inclined to say YOU haven't tried everything yet. Take another look at Chapter 6 to see to how extent you are still yourself.

You need to take away (Townsend says snatch away;) the key to your happiness that you trustingly handed over to your partner. You need to reclaim YOUR life. You need to change your attitude and your thinking habits before you can actually effectively! treat and behave differently towards your partner. This includes, first, taking care of your own well-being as described in Chapter 6. On the other hand, so that you can avoid being caught up again and again by your partner's moods and whims and sent on an emotional roller coaster, you must adopt a clear attitude toward your partner that is independent of his behavior. Why not see him as the person he actually is, at least at the moment. Namely, a person with a major character flaw who is quite indifferent to your well-being as long as he/she can assert his/her interests, who will consequently have to earn your trust again first, and who should be shown their limits and the consequences of their non-compliance by you quite urgently. If you adopt this attitude as a working attitude for the next time, then it will no longer shake you if your partner becomes impertinent towards you, for example. If you free yourself from the idea of what your partner "should" be, but see him as he actually is, you will deal with his behavior differently, because it will no longer surprise you "how could he again", but it will be more like "ah, that again". Believe me, the latter is better ;) And you can handle it quite differently. More about that later.

CHAPTER 9

THINKING: FRIEND OR FOE?

Honestly, I know this is all infinitely sad. When I write here: distance yourself emotionally. Reduce the importance of your partner for you and for your life. Look at him critically and objectively with distance. Take a "working attitude." We don't actually want to distance ourselves. We don't want to carry, do, endure everything alone. We don't want to distance ourselves from the partner even more; we want to get closer to him. We want to be loved. We want a partnership based on mutual love, closeness, security, intimacy, respect, freedom and trust. I know that this arouses resistance, and the thoughts: "why does this have to happen to me? Why can't I just be happy? Why can't my partner just understand?" Unfortunately, because that's exactly what he can't, and/or won't do. And that's why it's important to stay by yourself. I think I've described the mechanisms that made you feel helpless and have abandoned yourself to the point where you can a. recognize them and b. forgive yourself. You wanted to be loved, that's human. That's perfectly okay. But I hope it has also become clear that your previous ways of thinking about the relationship are not necessarily correct, because you have had these very experiences. As Nay puts it, "If you think something enough times, you will believe it." Even if it's for the ass (German saying): e.g., "I'm not capable of dealing with my partner's anger." Correct would be: "I can learn to deal with it differently". Think about the work attitude ;)

And what is the point of all this? The fact is we can't change anyone. We can't take the smallest step for another person. What if he/she doesn't change?

On the one hand: You remain by yourself, and are free to draw your consequences. Whether you continue the relationship, or perhaps seek happiness elsewhere. You have the right to be happy (if you ask me also the duty).

On the other hand: I have already indicated this. If you take yourself out of the equation, then your partner's system will stop working. That is, you can thereby make him/her behaving badly as unpleasant and not worthwhile as possible. And about it you can, in the less counseling resistant partners, initiate changes. The others are then left alone with their shit at their own request. Please be aware that this is what can happen. That you will give everything and your partner will not change anything. But then you should change something. Namely the partner. If your partner's problem wasn't so big, we wouldn't need all this. You would tell him/her how much things affect you; he/she would rethink it, and respond to you, or work out a solution with you that is workable for both of you. That's how it works with normal people like you. And that's why you tried for so long to speak to the mind of the ignorant, and it hit you full force again and again, how contemptible a person can be. Over and over again. Until you no longer knew which way was up or down. So, to make this stop: review your beliefs about the subject of your relationship (see above the example from Nay) best make a written list. If you find it difficult to formulate a correct alternative belief, just write down the opposite for starters, and modify a little if necessary ;)

Consider what behaviors of your partner you will no longer tolerate. For those of you who are also starting to lose track of where the top and bottom are, here's a list of things that count as verbal and emotional abuse:

- Humiliations and degradations
- Insults, disrespectful terms
- Intellectual games
- The concealment of information
- Questioning the self-worth of the other person
- Speech or action intended to make the partner feel ignored or not taken seriously or embarrassed
- Ignoring or threatening basic needs (e.g., the need for security by threatening a breakup because the partner doesn't like something about your behavior)

Write down the "highlights" of your partner that are not acceptable to you. We will then work with this in the near future. Look for people who support you in your plan, and are there for you, and can give you at least partially what your partner is denying you.

From all others please stay away ;)

CHAPTER 10

DO IT YOURSELF

I hope you have now debunked some of your false beliefs and thinking habits (in technical jargon, "cognitive deformations" - which rather vividly describes the problem), and replaced them with sustainable beliefs, so that you now feel empowered. Because now it's a matter of "doing the only thing that can bring about a change in your partner's behavior, which is to make sure that his harmful behavior doesn't benefit him at all."[14]

I asked you to make a list of your "highlights" of the behaviours of your partner. Now it is a matter of using these, and on the basis of them, clearly drawing your own boundaries and communicating them to your partner. This should follow (according to Nay) the following structure:

"1. When you said, when you did, when it came to ... (here follows a factual, fact-based description of the partner's behavior WITHOUT evaluation) so, e.g., "when you called me an idiot last night (fact) because you don't care about my feelings (evaluation/reproach - doesn't belong there!)"
2. Then I thought...
3. Felt...
4. For the future I wish... (Here you formulate alternative, positive behavior desired by you)
5. If you behave differently, then I will be very happy to hear you and make an effort to work with you to resolve things. If you revert to your old behaviors, then I will ..."[15] e.g. point it out to you, asking you to stop [if this is successful you should IMMEDIATELY be ready to resume the conversation].
Should this not bear fruit, I will end the conversation immediately, and take care of my business, leave the apartment for 30 minutes, move in with my sister for 2 days, etc."

Write that down for yourself. And now take advantage of the fact that our brain makes no difference whether you imagine something or whether you actually experience it. You are now doing so-called imagination exercises: "Imagination exercises are a mental form of exercise in which you imagine in your mind how you want to think, feel and act in a certain situation."[16]
So you imagine in your mind, how you ask your partner in a calm! moment for a conversation and present your new limits and the consequences in a very calm voice, very matter-of-factly and without

any great emotion according to the above-mentioned scheme. Mentally play through any resistance from your partner, and how you then nevertheless calmly and objectively return to your topic (yes, exactly, like a prayer wheel). You'll probably be surprised about how many emotions will come up in you while just thinking about it. That's why this exercise. Then, if you can play this out well in your mind, be sure to practice it with a real person you trust, who should mimic your partner's behaviors. Practice returning to your topic again and again despite objections, or if you notice that the conversation would otherwise escalate because you wouldn't be able to stay calm yourself either, adjourn it. This is quite important before confronting your partner. Be sure to take the time to practice.

It may be that when your partner engages in certain hurtful behaviors, you will have a hard time pointing them out clearly and drawing boundaries. If your partner yells at you or insults you, that is very clear, identifiable and nameable behavior. What about in the case of sarcasm, or passive aggressiveness, or when your partner uses aggression against you instrumentally? We will deal with that later.

CHAPTER 11

HOW YOU CAN TELL IT'S SARCASM AND FROM OTHER SMUT

How you can tell it's sarcasm: if you feel hurt, ashamed, humiliated, or degraded, it was sarcasm. However, it likes to come disguised as a "joke," and afterwards you're told you're oversensitive or humorless and there's no way it was sarcastic. This leads to you feeling even more guilty and as a buzzkill and doubting your perception.... Nevertheless, if it is not an isolated case, and your partner is not otherwise squeamish with you, then there is no doubt. When asking your partner to stop, avoid any discussion about your perception, oversensitivity, or whether you are humorless. Focus on your feelings, and that it can hardly be too much to ask that your partner respect them. Sarcasm, along with criticism, justification and stonewalling, are among the four horsemen of the apocalypse that can, according to Dr. John Gottman, reliably signal the end of the relationship. Because none of the horsemen aims at resolution of conflict, but only at devaluing the other person.

It is similar when it comes to the aggressiveness of the partner. If he is expressively aggressive, and capable of genuine repentance, there is a possibility of real change in therapy. If it is instrumental aggression, it looks really bad: "This type of aggression results from a deep-rooted personality disorder, and a person who shows this form of aggression wants to intimidate and control his partner in order to subordinate him. In this case, aggression is a means to an end and can be quickly turned on or off. Emotionally, the partner is not strongly agitated."[17] [R. Nay - Overcoming anger...] These individuals also show no guilt or remorse, and hurt others to achieve their selfish goals. Might be wise to reconsider that there are therapists who refuse to work with such people... I don't know why either... (speaking of sarcasm ;)

Finally comes the supreme discipline: passive-aggressive behavior. How you manage to be in the same room with someone and feel lonelier than ever before.

CHAPTER 12

PASSIVE AGGRESSIVE BEHAVIOR, WHERE DOING LITTLE AND REFRAINING FROM DOING A LOT ACCOMPLISHES A LOT

Ever had the feeling after a whole weekend with your partner that you never been so lonely, although he was physically present all the time? Have you felt guilty without knowing what you have done wrong and asked countless times if something was wrong, but "except" your "harassment" was nothing? Did you doubt your perception and feel frustrated and helpless? According to Robert Nay, passive aggression is based on denial. It is a nonverbal communication of the following content: "I am angry with you, but I am not showing anger and I am not going to reveal my true thoughts and feelings in front of you. Instead, I will do something you don't want me to do or I won't do something you want me to do to punish you, but I won't admit that either."[18] Aptly, Nay notes that this leads to being totally up in the air and completely insecure about one's ability to assess one's partner's behavior and one's own reactions.

In the case of the particularly immature persons, cold rage is added to the mix. The person then simply ignores you, treats you like air, and refuses to have any conversations. With very little action, your partner wreaks great havoc.

If you have any doubts about your perception, here are the unmistakable signs that your partner's behavior is indeed passive-aggressive. (I summarize here in an abbreviated way Nay, and he refers to Scott Wetzler's "Living with the passive-aggressive man")[19] :

- Your partner does not praise you even though you deserve it, and even when you ask him to, he fails to do so
- If you have done something good for him, he looks for the flaw in it instead of acknowledging that

- He "forgets" your requests, e.g. to do things or to show consideration, he likes to sow chaos, e.g. by not completing tasks assigned to him, or by leaving them unfinished, or by carrying them out so sloppily that you have to do it again yourself, or leaves you in the middle of the chaos, which has a negative effect on you.
- He does things that he knows very well will irritate you, and then assures you it was not intentional
- He is notoriously late, does not value your time and thus imposes his schedule on you
- If he notices your need for closeness, he keeps his distance
- Likes to delay things, e.g., when he realizes you want to talk to him about something serious, which prevents the conversation from happening in the first place
- If you ask him about important considerations, feelings, or needs, he answers meaninglessly, "Unimportant," "Forget it," "Don't know," while he may let you sense that something is very wrong.

And it's precisely this sensing that keeps it going, because you notice the contradiction and ask "is what wrong?" "So tell me please? Did I hurt you? What's wrong? Is something wrong?" And on, and on ... Your partner grabs you with these passive methods, because ultimately you can't stand the feeling of loneliness, and this knowing and not knowing that something is wrong creates massive stress by making you "guess" that something is wrong, but not what. And you react, ask, and beg for an answer... and poof; you are where he wants you to be.

How you can grab him/her even though everything is so indistinct:

Nay clearly states, "You are not a clairvoyant, and even if you aptly interpret the causes of your partner's anger, and require him to admit it, you are giving him to understand that his behavior is having the desired effect."[20]

So don't question, demand and sue for it: tell your partner that you take him literally: "nothing" is just "nothing" and that if he has something on his mind, he should tell you DIRECTLY and that you will then be happy to listen to him. Until that happens, you take what he says as a given. So "nothing" is "nothing".

Make yourself as independent as possible from his decisions, or even delays of decisions: e.g. "I have asked you 3 times to discuss with me where we are going on vacation, never the conversation came up. I am deciding this for myself now; you are welcome to join me. If not, then I'll go with my sister,...." Let your partner feel the natural consequences of his omissions; do not do his job in any case. For example, if he "forgets" something again, there will be nothing to eat, no clean shirts (if he didn't pick them up from the dry cleaners as you asked him to). Agree with your partner on time frames in which he should do something, and then expect him to do it like any adult.

If all this does not bear fruit, then you can ask yourself whether a person who has purely nothing to give you, who cannot give you anything, and who does not want to give you anything, really has to be part of YOUR life...

II. PERSONAL DEVELOPMENT

CHAPTER 13

"WHY ME?" II

Last year I wrote about how you can find yourself again in an unhappy relationship and how you can redefine your relationship(s) or get out of them easier. In the end, this year I will also write about relationships (because we only recognize ourselves in relationships - that's how it started here with the quote from Krishnamurti), primarily about the relationship to oneself, and how it radiates to everyone else. And if there is enough time in the year, then also gladly: "how do I live in a happy relationship?" would be something ;)

Last year, however, the most clicked post was: "Why me?" insofar you have encouraged me as my readers to write more about exactly this topic. So this year, we're going to take a closer look at what it is in you that makes you: *put the desire to keep this relationship going, or finally get it going, over your own well-being.*

Exactly.

CHAPTER 14

"GIFTS" FOR LIFE?

As I have described it, the mechanism of loss of control alone is enough "to drive a person who is in himself perfectly reasonable to the brink of "insanity.""[21] [Stefanie Stahl: "Jein!"] Adverse childhood experiences and behavioral patterns, however, can deepen this state enormously and/or make it last for a very long time, so that you waste years or even decades on such relationships... This happens, among other things, through the mechanisms I described in chapter 8, which bring out exactly these unhelpful behavioral patterns, and become an additional burden for you, especially if these behavioral patterns work against you.

I like to say that everyone gets "gifts" from their parents along the way that they never asked for and would have been better off not getting. But they are there, and I assure you they will remain with you until you finally "unwrap" them and consciously deal with them as an adult, emotionally leaving your parental home and making peace with it. In doing so, according to Monika and Marcin Gajdowie, you can make three big mistakes:

"1. Failure to understand or repress mistakes made by parents.
2. eternal expectations and complaints towards parents
3. (Apparent) rejection and repulsion of parents.

The last attitude in particular is deceptive because it holds the illusion of independence, yet this defensive attitude binds incredibly strongly to parents," Gajdowie say.[22] As a result, "both those who eternally expect [unconditional parental] love and those who reject their parents fall into the trap of emotional dependence."[23] This happens because you thus continue to respond to the hurts of childhood instead of acting as an adult and living your life detached from that of your parents according to your own convictions. The Bible already tells us this in Matthew 19:5-6: "Therefore a man will leave his father and mother and be united to his wife, and the two will become one flesh." There is no mention of "and they dragged the mother-in-law piggyback";)

But, all kidding aside, you're not you until you've left your parents' home and are no longer emotionally dependent on it. The tragedy is that it is precisely those people who had a particularly adverse childhood who find this step particularly difficult. Why this is so and what leads to it and how it still succeeds will occupy us in the next blogs.

CHAPTER 15

ALWAYS THIS CHILDHOOD NONSENSE

The fact that we feel this way, or consider it overrated to refer difficulties in adult life to childhood, has to do with the fact that we as children, on the one hand, do not have the ability to judge our lives and our environment objectively and distantly: "Mom and Dad have unresolved major problems with themselves that they are unloading on me right now, it's not my fault that they yell at me or hit me or ignore me or put me down or whatever. It doesn't say anything about me or my worth as a person; it only says something about them." Rather, a child relates everything to itself - really everything - and blames itself for it. In addition, a child who is permanently exposed to any kind of mistreatment learns to repress it, on the one hand to protect itself (because it may actually be a matter of survival); on the other hand, because it somehow still wants to get the love of the parents, because this longing is in every child. Thus the child adapts to the family of origin, even at the price of self-sacrifice, about what the child is of course not aware due to the described mechanisms of repression.

The parents are God in the universe of the child, and also of the teenager, even if it may look different on the outside in case of teens. And that means, you leave your parents' house with a complete control program for life: how it is, how it has to be, what is of value and importance, what you have to evaluate and how, what is your own value, how you have to behave. And this on the one hand on the level which was communicated to you and on the other hand on the level which you actually experienced. You are only conditionally conscious of all this, since you are completely penetrated by it, and it lies partly also under the veil of the repression. This is your MS-DOS operating system. When you start the computer, you see nothing of it. You only see the pretty user interface of your Windows 7, personalized by you.

I remember how my teacher once handed out a questionnaire with very simple "yes-no" questions. Like the question, "Does air have a weight?" The point was to illustrate how differently we think today compared to people before the Age of Enlightenment. With the knowledge of today, it was not possible to answer "no" to any of the questions. Looking at the sheet, two things became clear: the commonality with humans roughly stops at the fact that we belong to the same species. And we are deeply and unreflectively imbued with our beliefs that guide our daily actions....

CHAPTER 16

AND WHAT IS YOUR MS DOS LIKE?

I have written before that you leave your parents' house with a complete control program for life, this "MS DOS" working under the surface. The crux is, it was not written so that you can lead the best possible, self-determined and happy adult life. But it was written - especially depending on what your childhood was like - so that you might literally: survive it in your whatever home. And for no other purpose. (!) This means, however, that if you had the misfortune to have experienced an unhappy childhood with a lot of abuse, this program will certainly not be a help to you in your adult life, but a burden. To make matters worse, thanks to the mechanisms of repression and the fact that much went on unconsciously, you will not be able to see it (that way). How you evaluate your childhood in retrospect will occupy us later, at this point let us first state that problems of one generation deform the next and even the following generations, if the cycles in which dysfunctional families move are not broken. Because the children in the families, due to the mechanisms I described earlier, become co-dependent on the dysfunctional behaviors and part of a dysfunctional system. In their book "Mut zur Liebe (engl. "Love is a choice"," Hemfelt, Minirth, and Meier describe this kind of dependency with the term codependency "[which] can be defined as an addiction to people, behaviors, or things."[24] The term was first coined in therapeutic work with alcoholic families when it became apparent "that an alcoholic's family was often as dependent on his alcoholism as he was on alcohol. The relatives had not only adjusted their whole life, but their whole view of life to living with an alcoholic. [...] Especially for the children, this deformed life with an alcoholic parent was "normal." They knew nothing else."[25] Now before you think to yourself, "there were no alcoholics in my family, I'm off the hook, and this is "only" a fringe problem here..." It's not that simple:

"The concept of dependence and codependency today is no longer limited to alcohol, the whole realm of substance abuse is included - be it cocaine, marijuana, tobacco or heroin, [pills] - and other. This "other" includes almost any form of compulsivity, any behavior driven to excess. Eating disorders (anorexia and bulimia), addiction to sex, fits of rage, addiction to work, compulsive spending of money, an extremely strict and legal way of life, [...][compulsive washing, compulsive cleaning, the compulsion to hoard things...]-all these and many other forms of addiction are today placed in the same category as alcoholism."[26]

Because they lead just as much to the same result, to disturbances and deformations, which run like a red thread through life in an unwholesome way. And - if one considers the manifold causes - it is not a marginal group problem, but rather a plague.

CHAPTER 17

LOST CHILDHOOD

"Everything a person sees or hears has an effect on him. He automatically tries to find a meaningful explanation for what he perceives. If there is no possibility to verify this explanation, it [...] becomes a "fact". The "fact" may or may not correspond to reality; in any case the person in question will base his actions and opinions on it."[27] From there, it is important to consciously look at your childhood in retrospect and, if necessary, reevaluate it in order to discard false "facts" that hinder you and replace them with true ones. If there was maltreatment in your childhood, it is important to come to terms with it, and to recognize what beliefs and behavior patterns it has left you with. Here abbreviated following "Mut zur Liebe" are some different forms of maltreatment:

Active: physical and or sexual, but also verbal violence, shouting, accusations, insults, but also patronizing the child.

Passive: the parents are so busy (with themselves) that they are not available to the child, e.g. because of their own problems or workaholism; no attention, affection, no time for joint activities, the child's interests are not of interest, etc.

Abandonment: divorce, death, adoption

Emotional incest - child becomes a substitute partner, takes over functions of adults in the family (role reversal), can lead to physical incest

Unfinished business - the child is supposed to live out the failed dreams of the parents instead of being himself / partly also unconsciously (then it shows up as the midlife crisis)

Over-strict and authoritarian parents - the child is not given room to ask questions, it has not the opportunity to experiment, it has to "function"

Negative existential messages - e.g., "Instead of correcting a child's behavior, the mother blurts out, "I wish you'd never been born! You're just no good." This is nothing more than the execution of the child's personality."[28]

As a child, you are dependent on the love and approval of your parents. The good news is that now, as an adult, you no longer are, you no longer need it. I hope you realize how meaningful this is.

But as a child, because of this dependence, you did everything you could to fit in and somehow get that love, no matter what was happening in your parents' home. And this, in turn, as I have shown in the previous chapter, led to the fact that in some circumstances, in order to "survive, you developed a protective mechanism which consisted in "not seeing" what was happening" [in "Rozwoj" by Monika and Marcin Gajda], and also because of your experiences you formed "facts" which are not facts. See, for example, the negative existential message, a child takes it unfiltered as a fact, if mommy says it, it will be so true. You develop, to take up the terminology of the Gajdas, a "False Ego" determined by protective mechanisms acquired in childhood and the specific emotional, intellectual and social functioning resulting from them, which is accompanied by low self-esteem. A similar idea is expressed by the concept of codependency; you are a conglomerate of coping strategies that "saved" you through your childhood, but which always collide with the reality of your present and create problems, always adding new problems to the old ones.

I always find it fascinating when the same idea can be found in multiple sources. So we can read by Virginia Satir, in the context of communication patterns, where she points out four ways of responding (appeaser, accuser, rationalizer, deflector) that we learn in early childhood to conform, but also to buffer a person's low self-esteem. She says there is another way of communicating that is congruent, where thought, feeling, expression and action go together, where a person is whole with themselves. And she notes, "The congruent way of responding, however, is the most difficult to learn - but only because we didn't learn it as children."[29]

And that's what I'm getting at here, whether we call this "false ego," "codependency," or "lack of congruence": if you weren't lucky enough as a child to be lovingly supported in becoming yourself, then that's something you should make up for now. You should give yourself the love you need(ed). And here I don't mean some infantile "positive affirmation" or "positive thinking" (no use really, right?), but the maturation to the person you *really* are, and who sees himself *benevolently*, but also *realistically* in his humanity. Mostly, however, people who should urgently make up for this, they really get themselves down. Why this is so will occupy us in the next chapter, hereby the concept of codependency will prove helpful.

CHAPTER 18

NATURE DOES NOT TOLERATE VACUUM

Today we will take a closer look at two things: first, why a person who should "know better" ends up in dysfunctional relationships, and second, why it is so hard to stop this.

The first phenomenon is clearly described by Minirith/Hemfelt/Meier, so that I simply quote it here:

"In man, the home-finding instinct is not geographical. It extends entirely to the vast landscapes of our mind. Instead of physically seeking out the place of our birth and childhood, we try to reconstruct it in our present life. [In the relationship, at work in the superior/subordinate relationship, etc.]. [...] We bring our home to ourselves. We all have a primal need to recreate our familiar, family of origin situation, *even if that familiar situation is destructive and painful*. This is one of the most startling facts that a codependent must face."[30]

In addition, there is a way of thinking that is childlike, which the authors call "magical thinking," it is that sense of responsibility for what happens. [You remember, the child relates everything! to itself, it has no other frame of reference.] The child thinks, „'If *I behave this way and do that, this will happen. If I am perfect, mommy will love me.'* [...] If I wasn't such a pain in the ass, Daddy wouldn't drink so much / divorce Mommie. ',[31] This has an additional ugly flip side: „'if everything doesn't work out, it's my fault for not trying hard enough.'[32] " With this magical thinking comes guilt. [Wrong!!!] guilt and magical thinking reinforce each other."[33]

This results in a compulsion to repeat, which I think is rarely conscious, but all the more powerful. In "Mut zur Liebe" we read:

"1)   *if the original situation can be conjured up again, this time I can fix it. I can heal the pain. I know that I can!* Magical thinking. [...]

2)   Because I *was responsible for this messed-up family of origin, I must be punished. I deserve the pain.* [Guilt Trip]

3)   *Finally, there is the longing for the familiar, for security.* In reality, there may not have been any security in the family of origin, but it was the refuge of childhood - the only security the little person knew. Even more than a healthy adult, the codependent seeks refuge in the familiar. " [34]

It can lead to the fact that "besides the hidden desire to atone for the imagined guilt, a codependent can also be addicted to emotional pain. However dreary it may be, at least it is home. It's familiar. It's painfully comfortable. Relate the home-finding instinct to magical thinking and guilt, and you understand why adult children from dysfunctional families almost always end up in dysfunctional relationships. As painful, unhappy, even life-threatening as that relationship may be, it is, after all, familiar. That's why codependents so often end up in the very kind of relationship they once swore they would never tolerate."[35] That explains why it's so hard to stop. You're full of this shit and unconsciously feel magically attracted to it. But that's only part of the problem, haven't you "sworn off" more than once? Said "never", "never again will I" and then exactly done that "never" again? So, you became aware of it, you decided in an act of willpower never to do it again, and did with somnambulistic certainty as before, and if necessary chastised yourself for your failure?

And here occurs the saying of Aristotle: "Nature abhors the vacuum." What should have taken the place of that shit? What tools did you have to fill that void? What, of what you ever learned of life and practiced in your life, would have been of use or help to you? Wasn't it rather the case that, despite all your efforts, your feelings led you back to where you came from?

You may remember Virginia Satir's saying, the crux of congruent behavior is that we don't learn it as children. We only have the repertoire from our childhood. And if that wasn't helpful, to say the least, how would what you learned there help you through life?
Not at all. Exactly. That is a pity, sad, regrettable but also to be changed. In Paul's letter we read:
"When I was a child, I talked like a child, thought like a child, and judged like a child. When I became a man, / I put away what was child about me. "
If you were not fortunate enough to be well prepared in childhood for life as a happy adult, you must make up for it now. You will have to relearn many things, possibly everything. This is not something for that you have to additionally punish or scold yourself, or tell yourself to be a mistake. None of what has been, you could really choose. If you go at it again now, you will of course experience setbacks, and fall flat on your face in the process, and I promise you it won't be easy... but:

"[Karen Adolph, in her study "How Children Learn to Walk,"] counted how often children fell, how many steps they took, and the distance they walked. And the results give an accurate indication for the first time of how tedious it actually is to learn to walk.

On average, each child took 2368 steps per hour. In the process, they covered a distance of 700 meters, the length of about seven soccer fields. And on average, they fell down 17 times per hour. If we now assume that a child is awake for about six hours, he or she takes 14,000 steps every day and falls down about 100 times. "[36]

Now imagine that as a child you have given up after the 3 attempt. The trick is not to give up, even if it becomes tedious.

And I hope the blog gives you seven-league boots ;)

CHAPTER 19

EMOTION AND COGNITION

So a new MS DOS is needed. But how? If it's all subject to repression anyway, how do I know where to start? "Basically, repression is the "mother of all protective strategies", because ultimately all self-protection boils down to repressing the things we don't want to feel or don't want to admit. All other protective strategies such as striving for power and perfection, striving for harmony or the helper syndrome are ultimately in the service of repression. However, if I repress my problems, then I cannot work on them."[37] We must learn to see free of the perceptual distortion inherent in repression and projection. This is not easy, on the contrary, it is very painful, inglorious, and leaves us small and defenseless with our pants down. At least at the beginning. No wonder there are very many people who want to avoid self-knowledge at all costs, even if the price is very high.

Here is an example of how the whole thing works, if you keep repressing, quoted from Stefanie Stahl: " For example, Petra's shadow child [hurt "inner child"] thinks that she would be bad and that no one could love her. This felt inferiority, however, is difficult for Petra to bear, and it must therefore be fought off. Through this, however, it is not accessible to any processing. Now let us imagine that Petra meets Julia, whom she perceives as better and stronger. Automatically, but subconsciously, Petra now assumes that Julia will look down on her or reject her. Thus, she perceives herself per se as the potential victim of Julia. However, Petra does not reflect on this inner process either. Instead, her shadow child and her inner adult engage in a little psychological trick together: They find that Julia is untrustworthy and unsympathetic. They reject Julia. Petra's own perceived inadequacy is thus projected into a perceived hostility of her seemingly stronger counterpart.

People who, like Petra, have a high tendency to keep painful self-knowledge as far away from their consciousness as possible, are very susceptible to projecting their own unpleasant feelings onto other people. [...] Thus, feelings of guilt are also readily warded off in this way. People don't want to admit to themselves that they have screwed up and therefore project the guilt onto a scapegoat. [...] With these people it is also difficult, often impossible, to have a constructive discussion about problems. Due to their stubborn refusal to self-reflect, one is at a loss. [...] Sometimes the only sensible solution is actually to break off from this person, that is, to break off contact or, if this is not possible, to separate oneself inwardly."[38]

As I said, the price of repression is very high, because as we saw in the example, it is not fun to be Petra, nor to have anything to do with her (here we remember the title of the blog;). How can we recognize for ourselves if we are repressing? For this purpose, the emotions otherwise known as the "nation's leg-standers" can be useful to us, because we have them, whether we like it or not, don't matter as much we "work on them", or simply want to suppress them. This handling of emotions then gives rise to such artificial flowers as described above. They are there. One way or another.

The art is to work "with" them, because our emotions connect us not only with the outside world, but also (and this is very important!) with our inner world. Emotions can tell us a lot about our protective mechanisms. However, we should be willing to listen to them and understand their language. And that is already the next blog topic.

CHAPTER 20

WORKING WITH EMOTIONS

Or, in short, it is work on yourself. The more "difficult" show you, what you need to see and recognize and where you need to work on. Because it is precisely the difficult, strong emotions that come up at key moments of (possible) personal development. Here several things will be necessary, on the one hand self-compassion (not self-pity!), because you need to let emotions get to you in order to recognize them and understand the deeper meaning, but this requires that you can accept yourself with it benevolently, but on the other hand also humility. Because it is important that we say goodbye to the illusion "[...] as if we could walk around with a clean slate all our lives. "[39] This is how Anselm Grün puts it, and Gajdas go even further: "Introspection is usually unpleasant. And especially unpleasant in the beginning."[40] Especially exactly at the moment when you will begin to abandon your protective mechanisms, and recognize the truth about yourself. "Dismantling the protective mechanisms will cause inner turmoil, as places are revealed where we have been hurt. And with certainty it can be said that the first and most important emotional reaction that accompanies the recognition of the truth about oneself - is fear - with which sometimes sadness and/ or anger also appears. The

FALSE ME defends itself as best it can. The person doesn't want to know, doesn't want to hear, doesn't want to understand, represses things that are perfectly obvious to an outsider, the person locates the problems outside himself, and wants to change the whole world rather than deal with his difficulties."[41] Such a person, who cannot distance himself from his emotions and does not want to understand his feelings, lives only "on the feeling", that is, driven by emotions and not according to his free decision. Change is not possible in this way, neither is personal growth, the person turns in downward circles.

That's why it's sometimes helpful to bring in a trusted outsider who can help you look at the very things you're avoiding, because they're not subject to your repression mechanisms, and can support you in difficult moments to stay with yourself, and to look exactly where you don't want to look right now. So it is not about complaining in detail to your friend over coffee so that you "feel better", but about talking to a person who is himself emotionally integrated and has an objective distance towards your problem, and who would not hesitate to tell you something difficult for you at first, if it benefits your well-being and development. Because of entanglement and their own dependencies, family members and friends are not always helpful as counselors because of this. But don't worry, you still have to do the work on yourself. So how do I work "with" the feeling?

If you are facing a difficult feeling Gajdas[42] recommend the following steps:
Do not act - impulsive actions usually do not solve the problem, they increase it
Do not talk - "active silence" observe what is happening and what is going on inside you, so you can see more and deeper, do not look for solutions right away
Naming - important here - in writing - supports distancing, and increases clarity, you then literally see what you are thinking. Name the individual feelings, in which context they occurred, and how you would have behaved if you had followed your feeling immediately.

Talk about it - ideally in front of an appropriate person. In the conversation, focus primarily on what the feeling says about yourself, rather than about the circumstances triggering the feeling.

Act (?) - Only then you ask yourself the question whether you have to become active or make decisions, here the real work with the feeling begins. As you notice, you do not react directly to the people or events to which you have had reacted emotionally. These are only indicators of a problem that is within you. Of course, this does not mean that you should happily put up with everything from others, but this is *all about you* now, *your part*. That's what's going to keep us busy here. How you set limits and expectations towards people who obviously disregard your boundaries, I have already covered in detail in this blog.

CHAPTER 21

EMOTIONS IN CONTROL? OR IN THE GRIP OF EMOTIONS?

If you thought to yourself while reading the last chapter, "What is she talking about? You are supposed to not act, not talk in the face of difficult emotions and instead observe them with an inner distance? How is that supposed to work?" If so, two things are probably true: You experience emotions as uncontrollable and you have not yet learned a constructive way to deal with emotions. You have rather had the experience that feelings simply come over you and that you cannot influence them, instead you are helplessly at their mercy, or that your efforts to influence your feelings make them worse. The roots of this also lie in childhood. If you were not "emotionally picked up" by your parents in difficult situations and supported in naming and understanding your emotions and developing solutions, then you are now lacking these competencies. Unfortunately, there is usually more to it than that: „In such a case, however, the child can try to acquire these strategies by observing close people. However, the possibilities of model learning exist only to the extent that the caregivers have effective emotion regulation skills. In a family where the parents themselves do not have good emotion regulation skills, where the mother becomes depressed at every disappointment and the father reaches for the bottle at every anger, it will be difficult for the child to learn these strategies from his parents. If the child then continues to respond to negative feelings with his or her innate repertoire of reactions (e.g., crying, screaming, and tantrums), he or she may become a significant source of stress for the caregivers. Especially if they themselves cannot regulate their emotions, there is a risk that they will meet the child in these situations with devaluation and aggression ("You crybaby", "You little devil"). *The frequent combination of negative emotions on the one hand and the experience of verbal and/or nonverbal devaluation or physical and/or verbal attacks on the other hand builds up a negative self-image associated with negative emotions in the child. If the child then experiences negative emotions in the future, these will "trigger" the negative self-image.* This results in an additional threat to the need for self-esteem enhancement, further increasing incongruence. This is accompanied by the activation of additional distressing feelings, such as fear of others' reactions, guilt, or shame. *These "secondary" feelings then further complicate the constructive management of the "primary" problematic stress reactions, or feelings, and undermine emotion-related self-efficacy expectations."*[43]   Berking writes that this creates a veritable vicious cycle in which the "sense of loss of control [triggers anxiety and] activates avoidance schemes," such as [borrowed here from Berking:] situation avoidance (no growth possible), repression (suppression of feelings, which subsequently spill out all the more), and the activation of mental processes designed to distract and/or suggest control and/or "fix" mood in the short term (this includes the whole range of, e.g., somatization as a distraction).This includes the whole range of e.g. somatization as a distraction, worrying, rumination to suggest control, binge eating, substance abuse, compulsive behavior), which makes a constructive handling of emotions completely impossible, and the vicious circle solidifies.[44]

So far the genesis of the problem. Unfortunately, this problem catches up with us precisely when we are confronted in adult life with "events that involve massive *threats and/or violations of our goals and needs.*" [45] I would add: or with events that we perceive to be at least that serious. Indeed, such events trigger than very strong negative emotions.

In general, there is nothing wrong with this, because emotions have a warning function; they are supposed to show us that we are threatened. Due to their function, these emotions are actually transitory, unless... yes, exactly, we have not learned to deal with them constructively. Then it comes to the "experience of disorientation and loss of control and to the release of stress hormones [... whereby] with a too high psychophysiological arousal the cognitively controlled self-regulation is impeded." [46] Or even impossible (we are now thinking of murder in the heat of the moment).

Since our modern threats no longer have the immediacy of the saber-toothed tiger, and are usually very abstract in our minds, it is "easy" for us not to let the negative emotions subside. Anger that points out to you that someone has crossed your boundaries, for example, is desirable. But, "The moment you take action, your anger has done the job. Anger is harmful if you don't do something about the "annoyance" at the same time. You are full of turmoil inside and try to hide the anger outside. You swallow it without changing anything about yourself or the situation."[47] Krishnamurti also expresses it very beautifully: "Problems exist only in time, namely when we encounter a thing inadequately."[48] We virtually conserve the emotions and remain in a permanent state of alarm; the vicious circle continues to turn merrily on and on.

Well now you may say, ok, I didn't learn it any other way; it's pretty much solidified, so there's an automatic emotional program going on. So how can I change my emotions?

Barking says: "Patients should know that emotions cannot be controlled directly by will, but can be influenced by identifying the triggering and maintaining factors (perceptions, thoughts, goals, etc.) and changing them in a targeted way. In addition to these relatively emotion-related attitudes, it is important to build and strengthen helpful self-related attitudes."[49]

We can only start with the thinking. With your MS DOS [see chapter 16 and 17].

Because, and this is very important: ANY EVALUATION OF WHICH YOU! ARE CONVINCED! TRIGGERS A POSITIVE, NEGATIVE OR NEUTRAL EMOTIONAL REACTION IN YOUR BODY. And it is your own deep-seated beliefs, self-assessments, assumptions, and faiths that create the emotions within you. I discuss beliefs in detail in the next blog text. Let me say in advance: no emotion without a thought (even if these run unconsciously, you will then notice it in the negative feeling you have and should then consciously pay attention to your thoughts). There is a beautiful saying among the Gajdas:

"Thoughts are like sheep. They should not graze unattended."[50]

If you've been blaming others' behavior, circumstances, or exclusively outside influences for your emotions, you'll probably find it difficult to be convinced of the following phrase: "It's not things that worry people, but their opinions about things." Yes, that's right, it's from the Stoics. If you think this is merely a saying of crackpots removed from the reality of life, then I have bad news for you: then nothing will change. Because "facts and events are not as important as your attitudes and evaluations [and expectations] with regard to your feelings."[51] Then you will also remain a puppet in the hands of others. Because the responsibility for your feelings then does not belong to you. Moreover, it is, on the one hand, habit, and on the other hand, also more convenient to impose them on others or to blame them on circumstances. The price is then as follows: "You have no choice whether you want to be calm or excited. You have to react the way your old program learned in childhood tells you to."[52] You remain a "victim" of others or of circumstances.

I just mentioned expectations: the easiest way to make yourself miserable when dealing with other people is to expect! that other people will always behave towards you in a polite, appreciative, fair and behave in a considerate manner, abide by the law and not take away your right of way... nice thought, even if you abide by it yourself, you have no guarantee.

Anthony de Mello (my favorite thinker;) sums it up beautifully:
"The only thing you need to do is understand. Think of someone with whom you live or work and whom you don't like, who arouses negative feelings in you. I will try to make you understand what is going on.
The first thing you need to understand is that the negative feeling is inside you. You yourself are responsible for it and no one else. Another person would be completely calm and relaxed in the presence of this person; he would be indifferent to it. But you are not.
Then you have to realize something else, which is that you are making demands. You have a certain expectation of that person. Do you understand that? Then tell that person, "I have no right to make any claim on you." When you say that, you will give up your expectation. "I have no right to make any claim on you. Yes, I will already know how to protect myself from the consequences of your actions, your moods, or whatever, but you just are what you want to be."[53]

And Wolf and Merkle summarize this thought this way, „You got yourself out of the trap. The trap was that you thought you had only two choices: either change the others or be angry forever. But you have a third choice: give the others permission to be that way. The others behave as they always have, and you still feel liberated and calm. Take advantage of this freedom!"[54]
Does this seem very forced and around the corner to you? Then this is your thinking habit that gets in your way.
"Whether you think you can do something or you can't, you're right." - Henry Ford

Think about it.

CHAPTER 22

SHIT IN THE HEAD?

We're not used to questioning our thinking, and for the most part it's the right thing to do, because if we were to question everything when driving a car, for example, we'd be unlikely to drive off, let alone get anywhere - so certain automatisms are certainly beneficial in managing everyday life. But to stay with the example of driving a car, there are also automatisms that are burdensome. Let's take the classic example: You have an important appointment, you are completely pressed for time because your children took a very long time to do everything in the morning, and the slowest driver in the world is driving in front of you... Let's be honest, how long does it take before frustration gnaws at you, and how long before you get angry, and how long before you get really angry, and get uninhibitedly upset about the driver in front of you? Yes but, you might say now, it's understandable to feel that way, it comes over you, in the face of events... So, what does all this have to do with our thinking?

After all, we have here a triggering event, and the subsequent emotional reaction. In between, however, lies the essential step, and the crux is that it is hardly perceptible to our consciousness, because it has been "automated", usually through years of training. Let's call it the self-talk. And it has very much to do with our thinking. Accordingly, the sequence would be:

A. The triggering event
B. The self-talk - what you say inwardly to yourself about the event
C. Is therefore then the emotional reaction to your self-talk

A cannot trigger C without B. In plain language: No feeling without thought.

I would like to do a little exercise with you, it's very simple. Please close your eyes and remember something beautiful that happened to you: the last vacation, the birth of the child, whatever gave you a lot of joy. Please feel the feeling that comes up....

Unfortunately, it works the same the other way around. And, it makes little difference to our brain whether we are experiencing something, remembering something, or merely imagining something. The emotions inevitably set in.

But, if it is the case that feelings do not arise without thoughts, why do we recognize so little from these thoughts? Why can certain events throw us off course, leaving others completely cold, and vice versa? Why can't we seem to help being overwhelmed by our feelings?

An example: imagine you are standing in line at the checkout in the supermarket after work. It's been slow going all along, and now the woman in front of you is slowly putting her stuff on the conveyor belt. As her children are whining, she discusses with them the purchase of some sweets, which are then fetched at the last minute. In the meantime, it turns out that she has forgotten to weigh her fruit, so the cashier has to go and weigh it. As if that wasn't enough, the woman starts digging out all her loose change while paying...

If this situation causes you to become annoyed and angry, you will have to exert some restraint in order to consciously perceive your self-talk. On the surface, it will probably sound like this:

"Can't this go any faster? I just want to go home," "She can't control her kids at all," "Can't she do anything right?", "Doesn't she realize that she's holding everyone up, or is she just stupid?", "She's really getting on my nerves."

And you will get angry. You may have noticed that I have just emphasized that you will have these thoughts superficially. The fact that you have thoughts of this kind at all, and a corresponding emotional reaction sets in, is due to the fact that the situation in which you find yourself touches on beliefs that you have internalized quite deeply. Which generally valid beliefs can we derive from our example?

- Everything has to go my way so that I can be happy.
- I and everyone else should be perfect.

- Life should be fair.
- My unhappiness is caused from the outside.

What are beliefs? These deeply internalized, unquestioned beliefs are also called doctrines, and what they have in common is that they almost always take the form of an unconscious inner monologue. By means of these beliefs, we order our world in terms of causes, meanings, and develop our identity. They are passed on to us by parents, educators, respecters and role models in childhood. In the process, whole belief constructs emerge about how the world, we and others are, or should be. I think this became clear in the example of the supermarket checkout. We also establish some beliefs of ourselves based on our previous life experience. For example, a woman who has had almost exclusively negative experiences with men will develop the following generalized beliefs: "All men are bad," and perhaps also "It's painful to love," or even: "I don't deserve to be loved."
And therein lays the problem with beliefs. Our own thinking can really be our worst enemy. Our beliefs can be rational and helpful, and get us through life happily, or they can hinder us, limit us, and make us unhappy. Since, as we have seen, they operate in the background, we may appear to be at their mercy. And in fact, we are the most likely to notice their effects, not the beliefs themselves. It is therefore important to specifically question our reactions and thoughts in order to get on the track of the beliefs. For example, if you just blew a presentation and make it a matter of self-esteem, thinking of yourself only in terms of "I'm an idiot," you will discover upon questioning that you find mistakes unforgivable. Behind this is the belief "I have to be perfect." An evergreen among the unhappiness makers.

The beliefs are the "B" in our ABC scheme. They determine the kind of inner self-talk we have, and this is decisive for how we then feel in a situation. Now that we know what is behind B, we can go about changing B, that is, making B thinking our friend. And that means critically questioning our beliefs and, if necessary, replacing them with helpful and sustainable new beliefs. Let's take the belief set, "I have to be perfect." Serving 100% of an ideal in reality is impossible and inhumane to boot. Because it is a guarantee of never being able to be satisfied with yourself. Because if you actually accomplish what you set out to do, then theoretically it could have been even more and even better...This also gives us a yardstick for judging beliefs: whether they are hindering or helping. Observing the consequences the believes have for us tells us if we should continue to hold on to them.

So if we go through life with "No one is perfect - yes, not even me!" instead of "I have to be perfect," that doesn't mean we can't work on ourselves. But it makes it possible to let go and be content. A lot of pressure falls away when life is not perceived as a perpetual test. There are several ways to question beliefs:

For one thing, there is the story of the belief system: Where do I know this from? Who has always said this? Who modeled it for me?

Then the formulation of the belief: let's take as an example: „Everyone must like me. "

Really all of them? Does that always and absolutely apply? Could I use something else instead?

Another approach is to ask what is achieved for me by this belief set, the so-called "positive intention" behind the belief set. Here is the classic: "It is my partner's fault that..." - so we don't have to change anything ourselves, and are not forced to look at our share... It may be that you encounter an obstructive, but seemingly irrevocable belief set that you cannot directly question. This is where the exercise of "thinking the opposite way" proves helpful. Formulate the opposite of their belief set, and consider the alternatives that arise from the change in perspective. Once you have considered your inner self-talk in certain situations, and have uncovered the beliefs, it is now a matter of having a truthful self-talk. That is, to replace the previous self-talk B with D. The consequence of the new self-talk is a more appropriate emotional reaction E in the face of what has happened under A.

As I said before, it makes little difference to our brain whether we are experiencing something, remembering something, or merely imagining something. You can make good use of this to play through in your mind situations that you have identified for yourself as the "long runner" in order to be able to practice the new self-talk. Don't worry if your attitude and emotions don't improve on the first try. Be patient, the old habits of thinking are like a well-built highway, and you are building a new road. But it is worth the effort, because you will arrive at the destination in a better shape.

At the beginning, your new thinking will feel very wrong and strange. This is normal, because you are now going through a relearning process in which, inevitably, when you practice new behaviors and thoughts, despite the theoretical insight, the feeling still gets in the way for a while.

We think here of the alarm function of the feeling, say to it:"Thank you, that's okay, I take care." and simply continue with what you have recognized to be right until a new (thinking) habit has formed.[55]

CHAPTER 23

RUMINATION AND SELF-KNOWLEDGE

In chapter 21 I wrote that rumination is part of the repression scheme, one remembers an event in order to suggest control to oneself, this out of the unconscious wish that the situation may somehow please change. This is exactly what happens when one thinks over and over again in the same thoughts, words and phrases about something that has happened, or what one fears may happen: one cannot cope with a situation and does not know how to help oneself, relives it through the permanent rumination (lat. ruminatio) over and over again, and the negative feelings increase.

There I also wrote that *strong negative emotions arise in us when we are confronted with events that involve massive threats and/or violations of our goals and needs* [Berking], *or with events that we at least perceive as so severe that they also entail an extreme experience of stress.* I emphasize here so much the sensation, because it is our evaluation of the events that triggers the feelings, but we do not necessarily have to be aware of it, and yet it takes place.

There are those cases "when an apparent triviality completely upsets us and still occupies us days and weeks [or even years] later. The banal but hard-to-digest events that we brood over endlessly and can't quite let go of. That they affect us for so long and we feel so small and helpless so vulnerable?"[56] With which others don't take us serious, say things like "Don't be like that, it was nothing, take it easy" and additionally offend us and make us additionally feel that there is something wrong with us, because we already had difficulties ourselves to understand our violent feelings ourselves. We go around in circles and feel worse and worse about it and understand less and less. When we push the feelings away, they come back all the stronger, and we feel all the more helpless.

The perceived degree of helplessness also depends on your control beliefs; if they are internal, you believe you can influence your situation, which is desirable. If it is external-defensive, "you attribute influence to important people in your environment. These are responsible for whether or not an unsatisfactory situation remains stressful. They decide how you feel."[57] Or you have an external-passive or fatalistic control belief, in which case it is either fate, luck, or chance that is responsible for your life. But now comes the core of the poodle.

How is it that seeming trifles can get us so down? Exactly, because they aren't. We just don't see it because we're too busy pushing them away, letting others talk us out of our feelings, or feeling ashamed that we "can't control" ourselves and feel that certain way.

It is about more than the seemingly superficial situation, a so-called construct has been activated. "In psychology, constructs are defined as beliefs that have been formed in the personal learning history and are quite difficult to change. They affect how a person currently thinks, feels, and acts. Constructs color how a person perceives and evaluates a situation by casting information, events, etc., in a particular light."[58] "Once such a personal theme is activated, it creates intense stress that reverberates. Such personal themes (constructs) are the product of learning experiences. One stores experiences one has had in life and internalizes unfavorable phrases about oneself. These usually involve issues such as not being loved, not being enough, not being treated fairly, not having control, and being at the mercy of unfavorable events."[59] These learning experiences begin in infancy and are deeply internalized and little conscious. We only see our reaction to these deep-seated beliefs, but do not understand them as such because we do not recognize that one has just been activated. At the risk of repeating myself, but precisely because it is so important: „A belief set is a deeply held conviction that says something about our self-worth and our relationships with others. [...] Beliefs are formed in childhood, but they anchor themselves deeply in our unconscious. And so they are unconsciously carried over into adulthood as a psychological program. They have a significant influence on how we perceive, feel, think and act." [60]

To get on the track of this program, it is recommended to use the so-called funnel method[61] , where you go deeper and deeper into the feeling until the actual triggering construct becomes recognizable. You can also apply this as a dialogue, here is important: the listener must be absolutely trustworthy, and never use what he/she hears against you, because you will open up very much and thus make yourself vulnerable. Furthermore, the person should actually listen to you, i.e. not "stifle" your feelings, or know better than you what is going on inside you, or give hasty advice. The listener should follow up once, offer a summary if necessary, and not more.

Here's how it works for the speaker (if you'd rather just do it for yourself, be sure to write it down):

"Staying specific: Talk about a very specific, concrete situation that stressed you out and that still triggers feelings of stress: "What concrete situation stressed me out?"

Feelings: address your thoughts, assessments, and feelings about this situation: "Within the different feelings, which was the strongest feeling of stress?"

Meaning: Work out why the situation was so stressful, what exactly made it so bad. Explore the emotional reasons for your stress: "Why did this hit me so hard?" I would add: "What does this remind me of?", "Where do I know this from?" consciously think about your childhood. It is normal if you get emotional, cry, feel sadness or get angry, this just shows that you are getting closer to your construct. It is important and also helpful to recognize the construct: You understand yourself, you don't feel helpless anymore, and you can change something.

There is another important reason, the King's Reason, which Stefanie Stahl describes in her book: "Your negative beliefs are the cause of the problems you have in life, provided they are problems to which you contribute a share, and these are all problems except pure strokes of fate. [...] no matter what your problem is, it is causally related to your negative beliefs. They are your disturbance program. As seemingly diverse and complicated as your problems may appear to you on superficial examination, on closer inspection you will find that they can be reduced to a simple basic structure."[62]

And that is to be all? Yes.

But it doesn't necessarily make it easier, because the constructs (or beliefs of the wounded inner child, or shadow child, as Stahl calls it) are hard to get rid of. She writes "Even when we know about our shadow child and its beliefs, we are often trapped in its reality. I notice this with my clients all the time: They actually have all the knowledge they need in hand to solve their personal problems, but they keep forgetting it in between. In my opinion, this has three reasons:

1. The adult in us cannot believe that the matter of the shadow child is actually so serious.

2 We are so used to seeing the world through the eyes of our childhood imprints that it is quite difficult to believe in any other truth.

3. We shirk taking responsibility for how we feel and think; rather we wait for something to happen out there to redeem us."[63]

* The four basic needs according to Klaus Grawe: attachment, autonomy and control, pleasure satisfaction or displeasure avoidance, self-esteem enhancement or recognition.

CHAPTER 24

RUDE AWAKENING?

So, now you have done all that, analyzed your feelings and relationships, admitted things to yourself and critically examined your attitudes, and all that was not easy. Now, you think to yourself, it can only be best and excellent for you, a world full of fluffy cupcakes with icing is now waiting for the new you. Unfortunately, it's more like the Matrix: "Red pill or blue pill?" and reality doesn't have to be pretty. We remember at this point: that's why we like to repress so much. We suspect that what is to come will not necessarily be easier... we fear to fail, to be ridiculed, or even to stand there all alone, or to have to start all over again and that with an uncertain outcome.

There is no guarantee that all your effort and the battles you fight will actually result in success. They may be the only chance; but keeping what you know is like falling into a comfortable safe bed in the evening without having to worry much about it. It's somehow much better than uncertainty... also somehow it hurts less... In his book "Lügen, die wir glauben" Turman writes the following truth about change: „The moment you do something about your problem, you will most likely feel worse. [...] In other words, just when you try to eliminate your lies, the emotional pain in your life increases. This becomes clear when we think, for example, of an overweight person [...] when he decides to lose weight by exercising and dieting, the first few days or weeks are the worst. Not only does the person still have his excess weight, but now he also has aching muscles [and probably cravings for something he is now not allowed to eat], and he feels even worse. The emotional pain of someone who is overweight and trying to do something about it is worse than the emotional pain of someone who is just overweight. [...] Some people, at that point, it becomes too much and they chicken out - they go back to the [seemingly] lesser evil."[64]

It is different from the matrix in that point, that when you go back, you know that you are continuing to maintain an illusion. This is painful and it takes much energy to maintain all these illusions, but most of all it takes your life. If you do not face reality, and first accept what is there, and then work on it in peace, if necessary; you will always have to strive to put your art image over reality, and fearfully have to worry that the reality does not appear somewhere. And that makes about as much sense as trying to cover an elephant with a handkerchief, the biggest part somehow always peeps out... Furthermore, it is unfortunately the case that if you waste your strength and energy on filling your illusions with life, your true life unfortunately falls by the wayside unlived, since you can never act congruently that way...

Truth is so noble: if God would turn away from truth, I would hold to truth and let God. Meister Eckhart (1260 - 1327)

CHAPTER 25

ENLIGHTENMENT OR TRUE HAPPINESS

"When I accept myself as I am, I change" Carl Rogers once said, and he was right. As we saw in the previous chapter, repression takes a lot of energy. Say: "yes I have a drinking problem", "I cheat on my wife/husband", "I am jealous of the neighbors", whatever you have been explaining away with "yes but" and "with me it is something else" or "it is complicated". See clearly what/ how you are right now, not who you "want to be" or think you "will be soon". Nothing is harder than this seeing. Because the truth is, we don't want to see, we don't want to change. We want to hold on to the status quo but feel good about it, at most change it in our favor and then cast it in concrete to hold on to and never let go; but that doesn't work, "for life is a river that must flow let it flow" (Krieger, Die Fantastischen Vier), and yet we struggle so much, and so in vain. And then there is our ego, the great whisperer, who wants to make us know that there is something very special about us, and why we have nevertheless behaved "correctly" against our better knowledge, and so on and so forth. I have good news for you: you are not so special. Really not. You are not an exception to the rule. No one is. We are all just people, busy trying to hold on to things and make ourselves look better, sometimes even better than we perceive ourselves to be. It's just that we don't want to see ourselves. And I think that for two reasons: one already mentioned - our ego can't stand not being special. Then what should happen to our self-worth? Don't worry about that, self-esteem, when it comes down to it, will let you down too. The other reason that affects our behavior is also ultimately based in our ego: "One of life's most fundamental decisions is whether to see ourselves as fully responsible for our lives or to see ourselves as victims of events."[65] Let that roll off your tongue...you only acted ugly because the other person provoked you before, didn't you? Your ego, your self-worth as a great person couldn't admit that, for example, you thought you were right in your anger and, in turn, threw out things you never dreamed that you are capable of. At such a point there are two possibilities, you protect your self-image and the other person is to blame - or you see yourself as you are and accept it as it comes. There is nothing to prevent you from learning from it. If you repress it (the other person is to blame), you will continue to need a lot of energy to maintain your supposed self-image, and you will never be congruent because you are not being honest with yourself. How could you be morally right if you gloss over your transgressions? Kristin Neff puts it in a simple formula in her book Self-Compassion: Suffering = Pain x Resistance. She elaborates, "Suffering springs from a single source: the comparison between our reality and our ideals. If reality matches our ideals and desires, we are happy and satisfied. If it does not, we suffer. Of course, we can rule out the possibility that our everyday events are always perfectly congruent with our ideals. That's why suffering is so pervasive."[66]

We don't need perfection (self-esteem), all we need is understanding (self-compassion) - because this brings us closer to reality, and provides us with peace through acceptance (because the more I fight against something, the more I bind myself to it) and thus also enables real change. To change, you then do not have to accomplish anything, it will, when you are in contact with reality, simply happen in you.

Here is the result of a study on self-worth and self-compassion: "As expected, self-compassion was found to be more strongly related than self-esteem to stable and constant feelings of self-worth. We also found that self-compassion was less likely than self-esteem to be dependent on specific outcomes such as social recognition, success in competition with others, or feeling attractive. If we base our sense of self-worth on the fact that every human being is inherently worthy of respect-regardless of whether certain ideals are achieved-it is not so easily shaken. Further, the research found that self-compassion was less associated with social comparison and the need for revenge for personal slights than self-esteem. Self-compassion was also associated with a low need for bossiness. People who base their self-worth on feelings of superiority and infallibility tend to react angrily and defensively when their status is threatened. People who compassionately accept their imperfections don't need such unhealthy behaviors to protect their egos."[67]

What is written here above is a popular scientific formulation of enlightenment. Nothing more, nothing less. If you really understand all this, then you won't need repression, self-promotion, applause, a expensive car, or the plastic surgery, or the next career step. You can still have it all, but you will know what it is actually worth, and your salvation will not depend on it - why should it? You can just be yourself, and enjoy life despite everything that is not so "optimal".

Rick Hanson once said so well: "With negative information our brain works like Velcro, with positive information like Teflon". That's probably an evolutionary inheritance; after all, according to Eckart von Hirschhausen, we are the descendants of the pessimists of the Stone

Age. Try to cheat the pessimist in the New Year and consciously look at the (only seemingly) small joys of life.

I have once participated out of interest in the #100 Happydays - action. With the quintessence of this time I would like to say goodbye from you into the New Year.
Maybe you still need a New Year's resolution ;)

100 Happydays #100: so dear ones, now I have exposed you 100 days to the most beautiful or remarkable things, that happened to me on the respective day here on facebook. The aim of the exercise was to become more aware of the beauty in one's own life, and thus become happier. The conclusion after 100 days, in which all sorts of things happened, is: yes, you notice the light even in the shadows. Small things can be very big. Of course, in those 100 days I had bad moods, cursed at the idiocy of drivers, argued or otherwise felt disadvantaged by life... but the question also crept in: "is it worth it?" Are all the annoyances and worries worth wasting even a minute on?" After all, no amount of fretting and worrying will prolong my life by even a minute... And a feeling, hitherto unknown to me in its clarity, set in, no, it was actually almost a certainty, that underneath all the crap - which we struggle with day in and day out, and which we may cultivate ourselves through efficient rumblings and whining, whether alone or in duet - that underneath all the crap lays bliss. You just have to let it be. Life is a feast, and the tragedy of it is that most people die of hunger in the process. So: look up at the sky. Breathe the fresh morning air. Listen to the birds chirping. Go for a walk. Watch a good movie. Read a stimulating book. Help a stranger. Think of someone you love. Better yet, kiss him/her. Have fun... and I'm off to get something to eat ;)

CHAPTER 26

THINKING MINDFULLY

Recently I saw several documentaries about jealousy, alcoholism, and other problems. What jumped out at me was that the protagonists had zero idea of what was happening to them and had no viable strategies whatsoever to properly confront their problem. As harsh as it sounds, it was because they didn't fully understand and/or admit their problem, or in each case one got in the way of the other. It made me realize once again how important clarity of thinking is - and also, especially when you reach your limits yourself, a competent contact person. If one revolves around the same thing exactly the same way for the 50th time, then there is a pathology in there, and it is time to look at the problem anew, and/or to seek help. I have already explained elsewhere that one's own environment can usually not be helpful; it is either affected itself and equally entangled, or at least trapped in similar thought patterns. And how powerful repression and not wanting to be true is, I have already described abundantly. How can one actually think differently? Among the other ways I've pointed out here on the blog, I think Katie Byron's approach is pretty great. She says "I've never experienced a distressing feeling that wasn't caused by holding an untrue thought. Behind every uncomfortable feeling, is a thought that is untrue to us. [...] All the stress we feel is caused by arguing with what is." [68]

The problem is only that we consider what is not true to be true, or insist that things that are the way they are should be the way we want them to be. And still we would like to have things differently, which we cannot influence at all. Katie distinguishes three kinds of matters, namely her own, others', and God's. She notes, "I realized that every time I had felt hurt or lonely in my life, [I] had been in someone else's business." [69] So one question you can ask yourself to get to the root of reality would be: "Whose affairs am I in right now?" If they're not yours, get out of there. There's plenty to do with yours. To do this, Katie Byron has identified a set of questions that helps to gradually extract reality from the story you tell yourself. How to get yours: very simple. Write an uncensored rant about a person who upsets you emotionally. Write what annoys you, disappoints you, hurts you, what the person should change, do or not do, think or feel. Write what do you need from this person, what do you think about them. And important: write what do you never want to experience with this person again?

Once you have that, take their first set (and then all the others) and work through these questions with all of them:

Question 1. Is this true? What is the reality of this situation?
E.g. "My husband should listen to me." He doesn't, but he always should. The reality is, he doesn't. This is not about what is desirable, but what is fact.
Question 2. Can you be absolutely sure that this is true?
To stay with the example that all men should listen without exception. Do you actually always listen? There is no "should"...
Question 3: How do you react to this thought? Can you identify a reason to give up this thought? (And please don't try to give it up.) Can you find a reason that doesn't cause you stress to hold on to this thought?
Question 4: Who would you be without this thought? How would you feel, how would you be?

And then comes the reversal. Katie explains reversal this way, „This is where you pick up what you've written about others and see if it's as true or truer when you apply it to yourself. [...][70] There are three ways to reverse. You can reverse the judgment so that it applies to 1. yourself, 2. the other person, and 3. the opposite [this can still be combined with each other]."[71]

An example from her book: a young teenager who insisted and became unhappy that his family did not accept him as he is. A reversal was that he must accept himself as he is. And that on the other hand, he must accept his family as they are. [72] So everyone also sticks to his business ;) How much more relaxed it is when we are not struggling with reality. Then something else magical happens, or just something meditative: "No one has ever managed to control his thinking [...] I don't let go of my thoughts - I meet them with understanding. Then they let go of me."[73]

And with that I leave you alone now :D

CHAPTER 27

ADDENDUM: FORGET TO FORGIVE

As I was clicking through the old blog texts to get inspiration for the first text of this year, it struck me that I had not covered a topic I thought I had written about. Namely, forgiveness. I have often been irritated by the mantra-like conviction in the advice literature that one has to forgive "at any price", even people who have never asked for it, in order to be able to put aside any traumas and to find inner peace (the subliminal argument here is that one does not do it for the other person, but in one's own interest). This has always been a pain in the ass for me, professionally speaking. Because it creates constraints and a "condition without which it is supposedly impossible", which are completely superfluous, even obstructive, and incidentally makes the "frivolous" forgiveness appear as a shortcut for a complete healing process, which is wrong, however, and prevents this. Because one is inclined to believe that now I have forgiven, the topic is over. No, it isn't. Ticked off is when the responsibility for what happened is clearly settled, you don't hate your counterpart (anymore), and feel no anger (anymore), and have no need for revenge (anymore). When you have stopped the influence of this person on your life. In short, when you are emotionally detached from the person. Hate binds, the desire for revenge binds.

It wasn't until I read Susan Forward's book, Vergiftete Kindheit (eng. Toxic Parents), in that I found six magic pages (that's all it took) and even the term "The Forgiveness Trap." She writes that initially, as a therapist, she also adhered to the belief in forgiveness, but then, „I felt something was wrong when you unquestioningly absolve someone of their rightful responsibility, especially when they have severely abused an innocent child. [...] The more I thought about it, the more clearly I realized that this forgiveness was just another form of denial. [...] Some clients clung to their idea: "I only need to forgive, and then I will be healed. I get wonderfully well, and everyone loves each other. We often take each other in our arms and we all become happy." All too often, clients discovered that the empty promise of forgiveness was merely followed by bitter disappointment. Some experienced a period of well-being, but it didn't last because neither their feelings nor their family's interactions had really changed. [...] I have seen over the years that emotional and psychological peace comes when you release yourself from the control of toxic parents without necessarily forgiving them. This release can only occur when you have worked through the intense feelings of outrage and grief, and handed over responsibility where it belongs."[74]

I would like to add, since Susan Forward refers to the parent/child relationship in her book, and since the responsibility is clear, that sometimes it is also necessary, especially as an adult, to look at your own responsibility. This can also help you if, for example, you have put up with unacceptable behavior from your partner out of misunderstood love. If you take responsibility for this part, you will no longer feel helpless, and regain control over your life. If you have been deliberately and intentionally hurt in your life, it can be very difficult to drop the anger and thoughts of revenge.

I happened to hear again today a story told by the Dalai Lama: „Whenever the Dalai Lama talks about reconciliation, he likes to cite as an example the story of Lopon-la, a monk from Lhasa whose acquaintance he had made before the Chinese occupation.

"After I escaped from Tibet, Lopon-la was thrown into prison by the Chinese. [...] He stayed there for eighteen years. When he was finally free, he came to India. I had not seen him for twenty years. But he didn't seem to have changed. Of course he looked older, but he was physically healthy. His mind was still sharp after so many years in prison. He was still the same kind monk. He told me that the Chinese had forced him to deny his faith. They tortured him very often in prison. When I asked him if he had ever been afraid, Lopon-la replied, "Yes, I was afraid of one thing. I was afraid of losing my compassion for the Chinese." „This touched me deeply and also inspired me a lot. "
75

I myself have never been so impressed by a human testimony that it is really possible to be like that, even in such inhuman circumstances. I am still not sure if compassion understood in Buddhist terms also means forgiveness - I don't think so. I think it means seeing, largely unshadowed by one's own emotions, what is going on in the other person, and this succeeds in the case of compassion without the accompanying feelings of powerlessness and hopelessness. (There is an interesting distinction between empathy and compassion by Matthieu Ricard in his book on altruism). And this can also be helpful when it comes to recognizing how damaged and needy another person is, that they have behaved, want to behave, or choose to behave in certain damaging and hurtful ways. If you can see it this way, you may find it a little easier to not feel helpless and powerless, and to better deal with your anger and feelings of revenge caused by this person.

CHAPTER 28

BEING HUMAN LIES IN PAUSING - BUT THAT IS UNCOMFORTABLE

"There is a space between stimulus and response. In that space we have the freedom and power to choose our response. In our reaction lies our growth and freedom." - Viktor Frankl

And what does freedom mean? - "To be free means to be master of oneself. Many people associate it with the idea of freedom of action, freedom to choose where to be, freedom of expression [...] however, this conception places freedom primarily outside ourselves and completely disregards the tyranny of thoughts. [...] To be free, in other words, amounts to freeing ourselves from the stranglehold of destructive emotions, which always succeed in bringing the mind under their control, thus clouding and obscuring its original clarity in sometimes extreme ways. To be free is to take one's life into one's own hands, rather than allowing the inclinations born of habit and mental confusion to take the helm. When a sailor loses the helm, lets the sails flutter in the wind, and abandons the boat to the current, we don't speak of freedom; we call it "letting oneself drift." Here, freedom means holding the helm firmly in hand and setting course for the intended destination."[76]

Ricard notes elsewhere in his book that people in Western cultures in particular invest a lot of time and energy in every conceivable area (fitness, education, career), but on the other hand, "we do so little to improve the inner conditions that are ultimately crucial to the quality of our lives."[77] When was the last time you specifically worked with your emotions, on your thinking habits, or on your values? When was the last time you consciously examined/reflected/changed your ways of reacting and behaving? When was the last time you were in tune with your values in your thinking, feeling and speaking and acted accordingly in a conscious and chosen way?

I know I squeezed into the previous section everything from self-knowledge, to congruence and values and moral action, but without that, it's all nothing. Only in this way does everything really come together to enable us, in the sense of Frankl's saying, to really choose our response. At the same time, we live in a culture that makes it seemingly easy for us to get by without really living values. And a little insidious psychological mechanism helps with that, too. I stumbled across the idea in Harald Welzer's book "Selbst denken. Eine Anleitung zum Widerstand." In the chapter "Sorry, Environment," it says: "Environmental awareness and action [can be] only remotely related [...] the discomfort that sometimes arises from doing things that are actually wrong is decidedly easy to manage. People can put chasms the size of the Mariana Trench between their knowledge and their actions, and they don't have the slightest problem integrating the most glaring contradictions effortlessly and living them in everyday life."[78] The insidious mechanism has the inconspicuous name of "cognitive dissonance" and is, in principle, nothing more than repression with the purpose of maintaining a positive self-image. Here follows the description of cognitive dissonance from Wikipedia, as this article expresses the essential elements very well and in a concise but very vivid and lucid form: "In social psychology, cognitive dissonance refers to an emotional state that is perceived as unpleasant. It occurs when a person has several cognitions (perceptions, thoughts, opinions, attitudes, desires, or intentions) that are incompatible with each other. Such states are felt as unpleasant and create inner tensions that urge to be overcome. The person is in an imbalance and strives to regain a consistent state - a balance.

Cognitive dissonance occurs, among other things, when one has made a decision even though the alternatives were also attractive; when one has made a decision that subsequently turns out to be a bad decision; when one becomes aware that something one has started will be more strenuous or unpleasant than expected; when one has put forth great effort only to find that the outcome does not live up to expectations; when one acts contrary to one's beliefs without any external justification (benefit/reward or cost/punishment).

If the dissonance is strong enough, combating it can bring about a permanent change in attitudes and behavior. Strong dissonance arises in particular when the stable, positive self-concept is threatened, i.e., when someone receives information that makes him look stupid, immoral, or irrational. Cognitive dissonance motivates individuals to make the corresponding cognitions compatible, using different strategies, such as behavioral changes or attitude changes. If necessary, one's beliefs and values are changed, which goes far beyond temporary rationalizations. The term was coined in 1957 by Leon Festinger, who theorized both the emergence and resolution of cognitive dissonance." [79]

So instead of using self-knowledge to work on becoming a better person who is in harmony with oneself, one gets a "better feeling" via the path of least resistance - and that's it. An example, a very commonplace one: living with the knowledge of environmental destruction, practices in factory farming, the passing on of externalities by companies to taxpayers, and living under exploitation and at the expense of the Third World and future generations; in general, the fact that our T-shirts, steaks and the very smart smartphones would never be so cheap in life if someone/or something had not been exploited, tortured or destroyed for them. Soberly looked, it's hard not to be part of or complicit in an unjust system these days. We feel it. Since it's virtually "everywhere," it's not easy to escape it, and almost every consumer decision is affected by it. That's why we push it away, "If I thought about it every time, I'd go crazy/couldn't buy anything anymore/function normally in everyday life..." and we gladly reach for the new (thanks to the resourceful marketing people) climate-neutral, ecologically sustainable made from the plastic waste of the oceans sports shoes. And poof you have a better feeling. And "it is up to politics/companies/legislation to abolish the grievances, after all it is not us personally who exploit the planet, but rapacious companies and what can an individual do, e.g. a change in the law would be much more effective. There is no doubt that it would be. And besides, would the people of the Third World care about us if it were the other way around? Isn't everyone closest to himself?" When you think about all the ills, and you can't see the forest for the forest, and you come to the conclusion that you "couldn't function normally in your everyday life," if you think about it all even longer, and you wouldn't even know what to start with, you quickly feel overwhelmed, helpless and bad, totally frustrated. And that's why you leave it altogether to deal with it and stick the plaster of justifications on it. The more emotional you are, the faster this happens: "Behavioral researchers have also concluded in various studies that the people who best succeed in maintaining an emotional balance (by being able to regulate their emotions without suppressing them) also display the highest level of selflessness when they experience others suffering. In contrast, overly emotional people in the face of suffering of fellow human beings are usually more concerned with their own distraught than with how they can help alleviate the suffering they behold." [80]

But the truth is: "It is a shame for us, and all of us are responsible." "In this world of globalization, we have fallen into the globalization of indifference. We have become accustomed to the suffering of the other, it does not concern us, it does not interest us, it is none of our business." [Pope Francis - among others in "A Man of His Word", I can only recommend the film by the way].

I have often pointed out in this blog the amazing power of repression; as it is, things in the world stay bad because we don't want to feel bad (or as part of something bad). That's understandable, but without looking at ourselves and first accepting it for what it actually is, and enduring the feelings that come with it, we can't see how we really are and, if necessary, change something about the way we think and act.

So when I pause, analyze my own excuses and rationalizations given my consumption choices, and then leave them out, what remains is:
I am comfortable, stingy, and not really willing to seriously give up anything.
So if you'll excuse me, because as you can see, I have plenty to do with myself. Because I would like to take myself seriously again.

CHAPTER 29

#100HAPPYDAYS #100 FOR THE SECOND TIME: ABOUT THE FEASIBILITY OF HAPPINESS

"Why not repeat it?", and I am infinitely grateful for having done it, because I have had here easily 100 new insights, and lots of happiness and joy. Above all, I've learned a lot about happiness: it's everywhere - you just have to learn to see it. Getting out of the house in the morning and breathing the fresh morning air, that smells after grass here in the countryside, is happiness. To laugh heartily with someone is happiness. To stop for a moment and have a little chat is happiness. Going to work is happiness. Doing housework is happiness. Being on this beautiful planet is happiness (even more so in our safe latitudes where you don't have to worry about your life and limb). Since I can see happiness in everything, I can't stand complaining at all, it stresses me out deeply. I do not understand how one can have such a twisted view of reality that instead of being happy to be there and to be there, because every day is "world premiere", one can spend one's life complaining about some trifles, and therefore still miss the everyday miracle...

The difference between happiness and pleasure, by the way, is easy to see. Pleasure consumes itself over time. Happiness does not. Whereas pleasure can also be beautiful. There it makes the right dose of food, red wine, celebrations and shoes ;) Over the course of #100 Happydays, I've come to realize that what we love to say, only to immediately forget or dismiss as too small to be really true and effective, is genuinely true: happiness is in the small everyday things. We just rush through everyday life on autopilot so much that we are not able to see that. Happiness also has something to do with mindfulness. You should be on the lookout for it. You should consciously strive for it and look at the beautiful things in life instead of focusing on the negative. We can all do the latter automatically (keyword negativity bias) or as von Hirschhausen so beautifully said: "We are the descendants of the pessimists of the Stone Age." Because they survived, and we learned that as a survival strategy.

Happiness is doable. That's what I've learned. It's a question of attitude and proactive lifestyle. In the new German language of psychology, it's called "prioritizing positivity." In the résumé of Barbara Fredrickson's research on this topic, we read, "People who prioritize positivity try to do more activities they enjoy - monitoring their schedule rather than their emotions. According to [Fredrickson's] study of more than 200 adults, people who prioritize positivity have more positive emotions, fewer negative emotions, more life satisfaction, and fewer depressive symptoms."[81]

The #100 Happydays are a wonderful way to start doing just that. To open the door for happiness to move in. I wish you the best of luck.

CHAPTER 30

NEW YEAR, OLD DEPENDENCIES

Perhaps you have used the content of the blog as inspiration to initiate changes in your life and work on your personal development. Have you ever had the feeling that after taking two steps forward, you take three steps back, and ultimately feel like you're treading water? That the effort is too high compared to the achieved results, or that the results are too fragile, or that your environment can quickly make them absurd? Or that you will quickly find yourself alone if you consistently change something? Or you suddenly experience unjustified dislike and rejection from others, instead of others being happy about your change, which puts additional personal pressure on you, because you value these people and their opinion? Do you have the uncomfortable feeling that people who are close to you and from whom you would hope for support and positive feedback are pretty much against your changes?

For example, a woman who has wanted to lose weight for a long time, and finally succeeds in doing so, and wants to share her joy about it and her being consistent in this endeavor with her partner, hears something like, " Well, all well and good, just don't become anorectic now ..." Then you can't think of anything else, the joy is gone, and you ask yourself, why is he ruining this for me? And, maybe he doesn't like my change? What else is there that he doesn't like ... can I change without it being negative for me? What does it mean for us as a couple? Etc., etc. Exactly the same can happen to you with family members, here parents in particular, so-called "friends" and still many other people, e.g. at work.

You see, so that this doesn't lead to failing to do the right thing, it's important to be clear about a few basic, and initially difficult, truths about personal development.

1. There is no reward

Personal development is a reward in itself, and it is a perpetual process in which progress and, if necessary, a certain mastery can only be achieved through constant perseverance. Regression and falling down is regularly part of it, this is part of our human nature. There is no pot of gold to be won, no final goal, no hammock waiting for you on a paradisiacal South Sea island as a reward. It gets easier, but not in the conventionally conceived sense of comfortable. Still, it's more worth it than anything else, because what are you here for if not to be you? And no one said it was simple or easy to have, and it could be delivered from Amazon in 2 days. Or insured with a comprehensive policy, against all the adversities of life.

2. Your codependency and the power of habits

As for regressing and falling down, you should firmly expect it. Why? There's a nice illuminating quote from Ruby Wax: "Your brain is designed to keep you alive. It doesn't give a shit about your happiness." At this point, let's take up what was said about codependency on this blog, "It's a plague." Chances are very good that you are affected, because hardly anyone has the perfect childhood, and we all carry around something. As I've written many times, the more thoroughly we repress things or are unaware of them, the more we carry them around with us. Since as a child one strives to survive in the truest sense of the word, automatic reaction patterns and self-perception scripts have established themselves that served this purpose in childhood, and which are now habitually reeled off, even if they do not fit in with the current adult reality of life and are detrimental to it.

These run automatically until you consciously confront them and deliberately act differently than your habits dictate. However, in times of great emotional stress, the old behavior patterns can gain the upper hand; they are most deeply established. Here it helps if you are emotionally out of control and no longer behave in an adult manner at all: to pause. To ask yourself: What does this remind me of/where do I know this feeling from? What do I need now? What would be the adult way to deal with it? Accept regression in your development, habit is a powerful opponent.

3. The codependency of your partner

Keep in mind that your partner (if you are in a relationship) also has his issues. About disturbed relationships, and what to do, I have already written in detail, look at the first chapters. I mean here the "normal" partner. You get exactly the partner who serves your own weaknesses. *[probably the mild form of repeating unhappy childhood and wanting to restore it in new relationship]. So here you have plenty of potential for individual and mutual growth. But also possibly a problem, especially if you yourself are or have been dealing with a high degree of codependency on an imaginary scale: "Codependents develop a kind of antenna for the codependency of others. A person with a score of about 80 on our scale will unmistakably be with someone whose score is also between 75 and 90. Imagine a ballroom with two hundred people. One has a value of 85; all the others are below 20. A codependent with a value of 80 who enters the room will unerringly locate the other codependent in the crowd and walk straight toward him."[82]

In one of my favorite quotes from Krishnamurti, he says: "I exist only in relation to people, things and ideas, and by examining my relationship to external things and people as well as to internal things I begin to understand myself. Any other form of understanding is only an abstraction [...]"[83] The positive thing about a partnership is that usually your partner reflects to you very clearly what you are really capable of and what you are not, and he brings to light (even unintentionally) your sore points so that you can see what still needs to be worked on. In a partnership, it is much harder to avoid certain realizations and unpleasant concessions to the actual state than when you live alone. There the evasion is easier; you can avoid unpleasant things more easily and push them away for the time being. So a partnership can really bring you forward in your personal growth, because declarations of what you are all have a short life in a relationship if they do not correspond to reality.

On the other hand, a partnership is all the more susceptible to maintaining the status quo in order to avoid admitting things about yourself. Here is also the point why you may not get support from your partner or close ones: You hit (unconsciously) a sore point of the counterpart, on which it does not want to see. You change your role in the system and it becomes uncomfortable for your partner, because until now you have functioned in a certain way that is comfortable for him. I.e. a partnership can hinder you (if you cannot withstand the partner's pressure in case of doubt) from your development. This brings us to the next point.

4.   The path of personal development you go alone

No matter what the circumstances of life. De Mello summed it up so well, "The path of the enlightened man is lonely." And that is true. It may seem frightening at first, because we all have the need for love, recognition and belonging and security. I have also described these needs here. Only there is a difference between a dependent relationship and healthy reciprocity. If you are not by yourself you have no "freedom of choice".[84] The greatest discovery is when you don't "need" anyone to do anything because you are by yourself, and yourself enough, only then do you come to the embarrassment of enjoying your counterpart for his or her own sake. For today, I want to say goodbye to you with a text pinned on my fridge (just below the wedding photo, by the way;) Which brings us to the next topic: love and happy relationships. The text briefly and very vividly summarizes how personal development works:

The way
I walk down the street.
There's a deep hole in the sidewalk.
I fall into it.
I am lost... I am without hope.
It takes endless time to get out again.

I walk down the same street.
There's a deep hole in the sidewalk.
I pretend not to see it.
I fall into it again.
I can't believe I'm in the same place again.

But it's not my fault.
Still it takes a long time to get out.

I walk down the same street.
There's a deep hole in the sidewalk.
I see it.
I still fall into it ... out of habit.
My eyes are open.
I know where I am.
It is my own fault.
I'll be right out.

I walk down the same street.
There's a deep hole in the sidewalk.
I'm going around it.

I'm going down another street.[85]

III. HAPPY RELATIONSHIPS

CHAPTER 31

ABOUT HAPPY RELATIONSHIPS

"This time everything will be different", "She/he is the right one." That's how it starts, and that's as far as the thoughts usually go. Occasionally the impression is given that a permanently happy relationship is like a unicorn, you hear from someone who knew someone who in turn heard from someone else about a happy couple who were together for 50 years and still loved each other. What is not told is how they did it and if that can be extrapolated to all relationships so we too can live happily ever after. It made me think because, frankly, I too have never thought systematically and preemptively about conflict in partnership, or the practicalities of running a smart partnership. I haven't gone any deeper than the classic buzzwords like: "responsibility, respect, esteem, loyalty, love, intimacy, openness, trust, closeness, growing together (as individuals and as a couple), understanding each other, freedom of choice, reliability and security, and joy to share." - I didn't get there further either. How this shapes and shows up in everyday life, and should be applied in acute cases, the reflections did not go that deep. And then there is something else that probably very few people consciously think about when entering into a partnership, and even less about what it really means (I know that I am repeating myself here):

You get exactly the partner who serves your own weaknesses. The mild form of the repetition of an unhappy childhood and the want to restore this well known dynamics it in a new relationship. Because we unreflectively repeat what we know so far, and that is usually the reproduction of the relationship network from the parental home, with the familiar roles, behavior and the usual level of happiness (which has a short break in the high infatuation phase).

Furthermore, it seems to be common in our culture at least, perhaps because of brainwashing by the whole music and movie industry, to simply throw away one's brain in the name of the great love that overcomes and overwhelms one and against which one can do nothing. In a ridiculous short time span, a complete stranger from the street is handed by you not only the keys to your house, and access to material goods and your money, your own body, and very personal information, but also he is given the control over your own emotions. Psychologists explain to us, here a quotation from "Gefühle verstehen, Probleme bewältigen "*, that love is quite different:

"Love is a feeling you have for someone who gives you what you want. [...] A partnership or marriage can be compared to a company. The partners run the company together because they expect more from it than they would reach alone. The goal is to run the company in such a way that both partners win and the company is profitable for both of them. Both partners have their own interests and ideas about how the firm should be run. Thus, she expects him to fulfill his duties and responsibilities, and he expects her to fulfill her duties and responsibilities. If one of them fails to meet the expectations, the other goes on strike. He then fights for compliance and protection of his interests. If the other doesn't give in, or if there is no compromise, then there is the threat of termination or dissolution."[86] And if we look at the course of most relationships, it starts out overwhelming and magical, and ends with the dissolution of the company. So are we all dorky accountants who miscalculated? There's some truth to that:

in our culture, we are mostly emotionally illiterate when we leave our parental home, and if your partner permanently treats you like shit, it would be time not to set a record in forbearance and self-sacrifice; a relationship should not be a one-way street. Is this all to that: do we have an idealizing and overemotionalized view of the simple exchange of goods and services? I don't think it's quite that simple, because for one thing I believe that love is a feeling, but it can also be an act of willpower, and it is always a gift; it can't be forced. And it is only in our head: "Love is a feeling like any other feeling. You create it for yourself by thinking loving and positive thoughts about your partner."[87] I agree with the psychologists on that ;) But that also means it's partially decoupled from just my partner's behavior, so maybe that explains why people linger longer in something that's not good for them. Apparently, people can not only be "drunk beautiful" (men are demonstrably better at this), but also "thought better than they are" (guess who is better at this, but I don't know of any scientific study on this).

But now that we know that love is something that can be thought about rationally, and that starts from us, it would be good to think about it deeper. One more little thing beforehand - the wonderful saying comes to mind, but its source escaped me: "I had a wonderful marriage until my husband interfered." In all the considerations here, it is important not to forget that in order to be in a happy relationship, you need a partner who wants that just as much too and is making the appropriate effort on his part. Otherwise, you can stand on your head or cluck like a chicken, it won't do any good if he doesn't want to be involved.

I take the previous considerations as an opportunity to formulate a constitution for a happy partnership. Steven Covey recommends this in his book "7 Wege zur Effektivität", if you have a constitution, then you would have something to hold on to exactly in those cases when you urgently need it and nothing clever occurs to you. In addition, you make decisions thoughtfully and calmly and only once. So it's quite effective...

I have one principle, as a kind of basic principle - strikes me. I insist on leading as happy and fulfilled and as loving as possible partnership as standard, and not to accept it below. Of course, this also includes that the partner has not found his way into the relationship according to the motto "better one than none". The principle seems to be correct, because by Gottman (a true god among researchers of marital conflicts) we read: "The couples who settled for negative experiences in their marriage (irritability, emotional distance) were less satisfied and happy five years later. Those who refused to allow negativity, who insisted on gently arguing with each other when, for example, contempt or justification [with criticism and stonewalling the four horsemen of the apocalypse in a relationship according to Gottman] threatened to permeate their relationship, were happier and more satisfied later." [88] That's it for starters. Was that accounting, we now will have quality assurance : D

CHAPTER 32

RESPONSIBILITY AND HAPPINESS ARE SYNONYMS

Taking responsibility for oneself is fundamentally important for a happy relationship, a conditio sine qua non. Since self-love is often misunderstood, we say: realistic self-acceptance that is compassionate, but thereby allows clarity about oneself as one really is with one's strengths, weaknesses, and old hurts that reverberate. Self-awareness of how one functions, where one's sore spots are and their history, helping us to gain a true understanding of self. Self-care by realizing what we want and need and the self-efficacy to care for ourselves. Shitloads of "self" in a chapter on couple relationships? Not at all. In "Mut zur Liebe," at one point it says so beautifully that when half a person meets half a person, it doesn't give a whole, love isn't addition, it is multiplication (which makes it ¼, less than before). Except in the falling in love phase (note: no love yet!!!) no other person can make you feel better, and this is actually done by your projections onto your partner and the rush of hormones, and not by him himself. This fades away, and no one can maintain this in the long run, that you feel happy, except you. And speaking with Rainer Tschechne, we have some kind of happiness baseline (from childhood, sure) to which we always return if we don't make a conscious effort ourselves to raise it.[89] In plain language, if you are unhappy yourself, a relationship will not make you happier in the long run. It will add to your worries. If you are happy, a relationship will make you happy(er) or not. It depends on the relationship.

If you are in a relationship, then there is the added responsibility for the partner. How does that reconcile with all that "self" up there? Quite simply, the more you really understand yourself and the better you can handle yourself and take care of yourself, the more enriching/easier/better it will be for your partner to be with you in a committed partnership/ or marriage. Imagine not liking yourself, constantly whining and complaining, being prone to extreme jealousy, being disrespectful and not loyal, or even taking drugs, or liking to get drunk and be abusive, liking to cheat, or gambling away all your money, or accumulating consumer debt, or ignoring your character flaws instead of working on them, and not keeping promises - these are all things that can make life very difficult for someone who shares life with you. You need to take responsibility for YOUR behavior that harms or hurts your partner (and yourself).

As you can see, even before you enter into a relationship, you can do a lot to make it happy by working on yourself. God willing, you will then meet someone who also has a piece of this path behind him.

Because with a partner also comes his past and his old stories, with which you have to deal, and see whether you can accept them, or not. I think the reason why people in love talk about each other for hours or even days is because they want to be absolutely understood and accepted with everything by the other person. They want to trust each other and be the best of friends. It becomes problematic when your partner has clearly done things that you cannot morally accept at all (and let's face it: tolerating is not enough for a relationship), or when your partner is a walking bundle of problems, and these problems are by no means finished (be careful also with drugs, alcohol, gambling addiction or other addictions). It is also difficult if your partner does not face up to his or her past, and goes into repression, because then you will have to deal with the new problems that behavior keeps arising. It is even more difficult if your partner is still emotionally involved in old relationships (be it with parents or with an ex-partner). Also difficult are ex-partners who do not understand that it is over and want to force contact under all possible pretexts, because then they unfortunately become the presence of the relationship - here clear boundaries are very important. If children from previous relationships are involved, the love relationship with the ex-partner should be clearly finished, and responsibility for the children should be assumed in any case. They can't help it and usually need both parents. Caution is advised with "still" married people who will be divorced "soon". Quickly one gives there forever the second fiddle.

Especially in the initiation phase, people (and here especially men) reveal a lot about themselves (if they are not exactly pathological impostors, which can only be verified over time in the direct comparison of telling and doing). Stupidly, instead of listening carefully and thinking about what exactly the man is saying, the woman is too busy thinking about how she looks and whether he likes her. Instead of thinking about whether she actually likes her counterpart, and whether what the person is telling there makes another date seem reasonable, the focus is on all the wrong things. One is too busy with oneself and one's own effect than to ask oneself: what kind of person is actually sitting there in front of me? What values does he have, what is important to him? Does his behavior fit in? How does he behave, for example, to third parties or does he speak disparagingly about others? In his single guide, Henry Cloud recommends asking yourself the following questions, among others: „What qualities do you recognize in this person that, if you were in a committed relationship, you would firmly reject?" And "Does this person remind you of someone from your past? - Is that good or bad? "[90] And the most important question I would add is: "Do you stay yourself, or do you bend to please?" If so, my advice is to reread the chapters on personal development. Lack of authenticity leads to attracting the wrong people. "Authenticity attracts authenticity like wholeness attracts wholeness" says Cloud.[91] This often happens to women, but also to men, that (even if they are otherwise confident in their dealings) in a dating context they suddenly "act very differently than usual when it comes to something - more precisely: love." Here, a warning light should come on and you look at yourself (urgently!!!), especially if the counterpart triggers strong feelings in you, especially if you notice that you are too available for a newly met person, or feel emotionally dependent on him, and he can strongly influence you. There's this great saying, "Follow your heart, but don't forget your brain." In the case of initiating a relationship, it is tremendously important to prioritize values over feelings. No "He will change for me.", "He surely doesn't mean it..." or "She absolutely needs my help, only I can help her." - unfortunately, when dating, many also often confuse "problematic" with "interesting" and get drawn into very unhealthy relationships. If you're already seeing smoke on the first few dates, run. AWAY. The end. Don't go looking to see if it's really burning or how bad. It can save a lot of doom and gloom. Steve Santagati advises in his book "Mannual" to make a dealbreaker list. In writing. In order to have a clear rational guideline and decision basis in emotional confusions, as they can arise. He says it very clearly: "You have to be ready to just walk away if the deal is no good. If you find it hard now, think how hard it will be after a relationship that's been messed up for months or years. [...] If you have to question your rules/standards, better let the deal go! "[92] This is also how you take responsibility for your happiness and well-being. How to do that together with someone in a relationship comes in the next chapters.

CHAPTER 33

POSITIVITY - WHAT WISE MEN SAY ABOUT HAPPY RELATIONSHIPS (AS IT TURNED OUT WHILE WRITING)

In the case of a relationship initiation, it was advisable to see that you do not forget your values in the rush of being in love, and pay special attention to yourself when the relationship becomes serious. Because the moment it starts to be "about something important, namely love" for you, it can happen that even if you were a consolidated single, now old relationship behavior patterns (of course also learned from childhood and possibly consolidated in later relationships) kick in, and put you to a hard test. As long as you haven't established new ones, the old ones will inevitably kick in automatically (!). The mean thing is that it happens unconsciously and imperceptibly. If you are still confident with yourself in the initiation phase, everything can change as soon as it becomes "important" for you. Pay special attention to yourself during this time. I may be repeating myself here, but this is especially important and since it happens insidiously and thus mostly unnoticed, it is especially insidious.

But now we want to look at existing relationships, where the longed-for, only true, dearest and best special person... yes what actually? Has degenerated into an additional annoying burden in the stress of everyday life? To the guy who never cuts his toenails, and constantly "forgets" the garbage. To the chick who's always oiling the wheels, never satisfied, and practically never stops talking?

There was something: „While freshly in love couples [...] everyday interactions are usually very positive, attentive, interested, caring, supportive and reinforcing towards the partner, these niceties are often lost in the course of the partnership, especially under stress."[93] And a short time later, unfortunately, it looks particularly bad for the supposedly most important person: „Stress demonstrably reduces positive behaviors in everyday life, and this most strongly in the partnership or family. In no other social context do people allow themselves so much to leave their politeness out of it, as in couple and family relationships; here one shows oneself much more critical, gruff, irritable and indignant. Here, people allow themselves to behave in ways that they would never dare to show in public."[94]

Yet the partnership should actually be the place "where people can open up to each other and talk about feelings and experiences in an intimate way. This emotional exchange not only forms the basis for a sustainable partnership, it is also an expression of an exclusive relationship, as only a close partnership can be. Several studies show that the relationship partner is the most important caregiver, and even close friends do not come close to achieving this status as a support resource. In most cases, the partner is the only person to whom one can confide unconditionally, given the appropriate quality of the relationship, and with whom one can find the support one needs." [95]

Gottman makes it sound like this: „Friendship keeps the flame of love burning. [...] And the "preponderance of positive feelings"[is also very conducive to love]. The positive thoughts they have for each other and their marriage are so convincing that they outweigh the negative feelings. [...] They assume that their lives together will be successful and, in case of doubt, always opt for the marriage-preserving solution."[96]

You may remember, the topic was quality assurance ;) The above seems totally utopian and idealistic to you? Could it also be due to you?

Here is another statement from Christian Thiel, on the subject of "Happy Relationship", which questions exactly that: „If you do not think positively about your partner, then you should seriously consider whether you are in the right relationship. That's one possibility, there's a second. *It's quite possible that you simply have absurd ideas about love. Many couples have that. They believe it is possible to criticize their partner incessantly and think badly of him or her just as often - and at the same time be a loving couple.* This is a fatal misconception. Many couples pay for it with the loss of their love." [97] So what to do?

On this topic now a quote from Arnold Retzer in "Lob der Vernunftehe". In the chapter 'Illusions create reality' he writes: "Positive illusions change both partners. If we see the good sides in others, this has a direct effect on how we see and feel ourselves. It's quite easy to feel comfortable assuming you have the ideal partner!" And here's the best part: " On the other hand, over time, your partner takes on the image you have of him or her. At some point, you yourself believe that you are as beautiful and generous and funny as the other person thinks you are, and you do everything you can to confirm that image. So the illusion can also create realities in marriage."[98] (Attention. Capital assholes and narcissists excluded, read the first chapters of the blog for this).

Creating realities succeeds particularly well in marriage: "If we compare the attribution of strengths and positive characteristics made by close friends and spouses, we find that satisfied couples find more positives in their partners than even close friends do. However, among dissatisfied couples, partners also see more negatives in each other than do close friends. Couples thus draw the line wider than others for both positive and negative illusions. They exaggerate in both the positive and the negative."[99]

Now you know how the "best greatest and dearest man in the world" and "best most beautiful and greatest woman in the world" comes about, and is meant honestly to boot. And this despite the fact that there are 7.67 billion people in the world. It starts in your head. In what you think, what you say, how you behave and of course how your counterpart deals with it. The magic word is positivity. Gottman states: „Affection and admiration are two of the most important components of a fulfilling and long-lasting relationship. Even though happily married couples sometimes want to despair over their partners' quirks, they still feel that the person they married is worth honoring and respecting."[100] And Thiel notes, „There is no doubt that most relationships go off the rails because they lack recognition, appreciation and respect. Both partners are extremely emotionally malnourished. They are lacking - a good word."[101]

And how this works, with the good words, you can read in the next chapter - talk nice to me.

CHAPTER 34

TALK NICE TO ME

If your partner sarcastically nags you, that's his immaturity. If you retort in the same way, that's where your immaturity begins. One of the basic secrets of successful communication is nothing more "[...] than displaying good manners. That means treating your partner with the same respect that you give to strangers. [...] And he has by no means vowed to spend his life with you."[102] So, we're all clear then. Not quite, I'm afraid. Because talking is hard, for example, we are rarely are in dialogue, This sad truth can be read in Emotion Selling by Gerhard Bittner, he comes to the following conclusion: "People talk little to *each other*. "[103] And Marshall Rosenberg packs a punch: "In my study of what alienates us from our empathetic nature, I have identified specific forms of language and communication that I believe contribute to our violent behavior toward ourselves and others. By the term "life-alienating communication," I mean these forms of communication.[2104]

And yes, we mainly learn these. For example: "The more we have blamed others in the past, suspected them, punished them or made them feel guilty because they did not respond to our requests as we wished, the greater the likelihood that our requests will now be perceived as demands. We also pay for it when others use such tactics. The more massively people in our lives have been blamed, punished, or pushed to feel guilty for not doing what others wanted them to do, the more likely they are to carry that burden into their continuing relationships and hear a demand in every request."[105] I think most find themselves in this type of communication. By the way, you can tell if it was a request by the reaction when it was refused/not fulfilled.

If people were aware of how much damage their unthoughtful talk causes, they would simply shut up more often. The damage that occurs is psychological, but also physical, and this can even be measured: "For example, a negatively associated word such as the word "problem" always and without exception triggers a measurable stress reaction in a person's body. By activating the stress hormones, this means damage to the organism. In medicine, it is now considered proven by valid studies that negative communication causes psychological defense reactions and avoidance reactions."[106]

This has a great significance for conversations in relationships: "With every second of communication in a negative emotional state, unfortunately, the account of negative emotion in the partner's head grows. *Especially the little things count.* If the evening greeting often changes from "I'm glad to see you" (positive emotion value) to "Are you there already?" (negative emotion value), then the brain recognizes the reproach behind it and gives the search command: Search me all unfriendly greetings with reproachful undertone. Our research has shown that we hear an average of 500 negative remarks per day. The cost-benefit theory of social interaction now describes that the *greater frequency and stronger impact of negative communication makes contact with the other increasingly less worthwhile*. The positive feeling simply becomes less and less. We speak of attrition-communication. Attrition-communication means: when relationships, whether private or professional, become worse day by day due to the predominantly negative communication, negative remarks, telling of annoyances and problems, disagreements and many other things. In the long run, this process often leads to the end of contact and the relationship."[107]

So you can bring about the end of your relationship by banalities. The quicker way is to criticize. I like to say it very clearly: Criticism sucks and is useless on top of that, when it comes about bringing change, but very effective in widening the gap between each other and adding a huge shovel of negativity to the relationship account. All you can do is express your understanding of your partner's behavior, and ask them to do things. "[...] it is the only approach that works. It is a simple fact that people can change only when they feel that you basically love and accept them as they are. Those who feel criticized, unloved and unwanted cannot change. Instead, the partner feels pressured and focuses on defending himself."[108]

I sincerely hope that, considering these facts, you will prefer to keep your mouth shut more often, especially when you have nothing nice to say, for the sake of your relationship. For our culture it means to learn communication completely new. Bittner shows in his book that the ratio of criticism to praise is 90:10[109] , and Gottman has become known with the 5:1 formula, namely that it takes 5 times of praise to outweigh 1 time of criticism. The negative weighs much more heavily and most relationship accounts of longer relationships are likely to tend to be negative simply because of negative communication habits.

"For many couples, an unexpected difference in their relationship is revealed when they realize that they shouldn't take their day-to-day togetherness for granted. Remember that helping each other on a daily basis will do more for the strength and passion in your marriage than going to the Bahamas for two weeks."[110]

It is also important and helpful to keep in mind the following fact about conflict in relationships: " Psychologist Dan Wile said it most aptly in his book: Partnership Problems-No Problem: > when you choose a partner for life (...) you will inevitably also choose a certain number of unsolvable problems that you will then have to struggle with for the next ten, twenty, or fifty years.< Your marriage will be successful as long as the problems you choose are such that you can deal with them."[111] "[Even] neuroses need not necessarily cause a marriage to fail [...] If you can accept each other's alienating sides and deal with them with care, affection, and respect, your marriage will endure."[112]

The problems begin when you perceive the partner's behavior as a threat to the relationship, and he steadfastly refuses to change anything. Here it is necessary to make clear your own point of view, including all beliefs, fears and feelings, and if this is not taken into account by the partner in any form, to draw the consequences for yourself. In less drastic cases of insoluble conflicts, such an open discussion about what is going on in one's mind about a certain topic and why it is so important can help to better accept the partner as he or she is, or even to achieve a partial rapprochement through better understanding of the other's respective motives and motivations, or simply to be able to handle the disagreement more easily. They may also disagree, and still love and respect each other. The funneling method presented in chapter ... is helpful when you need clarity about the hidden level of a conflict issue, this is especially helpful when you are arguing bitterly and don't quite understand why yourself. "[I can] assure you that most arguments are really not about whether the toilet seat is up or down, or whose turn it is to take out the trash. There are deeper, hidden issues that fuel these superficial conflicts, making them seem much stronger and more hurtful than they otherwise would be."[113]

In order for you to better resolve conflicts, it is important to burst a few illusions that one may have regarding (usually still young, later it comes on its own) relationships:

- Your partner will hurt you
- He will do it exactly where you have already been hurt in your childhood and developed the naive idea that the one/one would not do this
- Your partner will behave selfishly
- He will not take things that are of special importance to you seriously, because they have no such meaning for him, and consequently he does not feel it and cannot comprehend it.
- Your partner will not support you in matters that are important to you, or even criticize you for them or make fun of them
- He will criticize you basically
- He will disappoint you
- He will not fulfill or keep things he has promised to do
- He will not respond to your needs, but will complain loudly if you do not meet his
- He will demand praise from you, and be stingy with it himself
- He will get on nerves and make you white-hot
- He will fart in your presence
- He will tell the same story for the hundredth time

If this happens rather very rarely, there is more right than wrong with your partner. He is only human. Like you. And you will do all this too. That's why, in the time in between, it's important to look at each other with love and goodwill, to take time for each other, and to respond to the other person, giving them as much praise, love and appreciation as you possibly can. Have you ever noticed that people who don't feel empathically heard are constantly repeating themselves? I stumbled across this in Rosenberg's NVC, it's true. Pay attention to repetition. Also in the argument, there your partner is probably missing that you have not accepted him with the pain that (probably you) have caused. Have not appreciated and acknowledged the pain. But only then the pain can leave. This is a very hard exercise because we want to get away from it rather than there, especially when we are the one causing it. Talk openly with each other about what you feel; what scares you, what you need. Many people don't realize what they actually need, but rather what they don't want. Sometimes we talk for the sake of talking. Since we've seen how damaging negative communication is, ask yourself: do I really need my partner's support and empathy right now, or am I letting my relationship degenerate into a mental-emotional dumping ground? Can I help myself?

When you realize that you need your partner, tell him. And how you need him. Listening, compassion. Understanding, acceptance. No one really needs advice (I always wonder why they like to give it so much? To shorten the emotional sermon, and because one feels obliged to solve the other's problems?) This only creates another problem. The partner feels that you are not "there", and want to fob him off quickly with "solutions". Be there, listen, "take an "us vs. them" attitude [with your partner]."[114] Be loyal to your partner. This is an essential element, Gottman formulates it here for what he considers to be actually the most difficult relationship (mother-in-law vs. daughter-in-law) whereas I find it applies to all other relatives, friends and acquaintances, actually all people: " [...] it must be remembered that one of the most fundamental tasks of marriage is to create a sense of "we" between husband and wife. So the husband needs to let his mother know that his wife does indeed come first. "[115] Don't throw away your sense of togetherness because you want to pander somewhere, or would like to be proven right "from the outside." You certainly wouldn't want your partner to do the same.

If you quarrel, and it will happen, try to remember that you actually love each other, and want to be together. Do not look for the culprit, but for a solution or a compromise. If you already start abruptly, can't accept your partner's appeasements and placations, or even criticism, contempt and justification take hold, or one of you starts stonewalling[116] save what can be saved and take a break. "If your heart rate exceeds 100 beats per minute, you won't be able to hear what your partner is trying to tell you, no matter how hard you try. Take a break for 20 minutes before continuing.[117] Separate yourself physically, distract yourself mentally. When you leave the house, make a clear announcement of when you will return and, most importantly, stick to it. Accept that your partner needs longer, needs distance, or needs to repeat himself three more times until it's good again.

I wish you that there is always one in the dispute who manages to be "the more adult one on duty" and who pulls the break.

Avoid staying pregnant with your resentment for long. Things don't get better if you let them ferment. But make very clear announcements. The other day, a woman complained to me that her husband had completely overridden her, not accepting that she had actually said "no." The problem was: she didn't say it. She thought he could interpret it from the lines of her drivel. He couldn't.

Whatever you're doing in your relationship, I'd like to leave you with one last piece of biblical advice (the best for last):

"Do not let the sun go down while you are still angry." (Eph. 4:26)

EPILOG

Lao Tzu said, "He who knows others is smart. He who knows himself is wise." I also understood very late how much psychology is useful in this. In this respect, I have changed from Saul to Paul in my dealings with psychology.

Psychology provides the insight and tools, some of which are described in this book, to really understand yourself. When your car breaks down, you don't just tinker with it without a clue and see what happens, do you? Why are we then inclined to do that with our lives? Why do we shy away so much from expert opinion here? Why is help so frowned upon here, even though we otherwise drive to the repair shop or take the aching tooth to the dentist without a hitch?

My basic insight is (and here I share the opinion of Stefanie Stahl, see quote at the end of chapter 23) that we do not want to admit certain things:

1. That it all lies in childhood (and traumatic difficult experiences in adulthood, if applicable).
2. That we are so imbued with it that it doesn't occur to us in everyday life that there could be something wrong with our perception.
3. Or that we think our problems are so special that the "easy methods" don't help anyway
4. Whereby this is also only an ingenious attempt to evade responsibility for oneself
5. And to avoid having to change anything
6. Because we fear the unknown more than the known pain.

But it is as simple as that. Do you sometimes feel that people around you (be they family members, politicians, heads of state) behave in a totally childish way? That is an expression of it. Only that unfortunately it's no longer about the shovel in the sandbox, but the behavior remains the same.

I hope you realize how important it is to really look at yourself, rather than reel off an imposed program.
You will also find that the absence of suffering does not mean a happy and fulfilled life. However, it is a necessary condition when you are trapped in pathological patterns, because otherwise they will keep pulling you down. That is why it is so important to free yourself from them.

There are still a trillion things that can be said about it, for which the space in this book is not sufficient. There are countless fascinating findings in psychology, which for (unfortunately) not so long have been dealing not only with the healing of diseases, but also with how to live a fulfilled life and what happiness is all about. Perhaps this will be the subject of a next book.

I wish you a good time.

BIBLIOGRAPHY AND REFERENCES

Note on quotations: my insertions /changes or omissions [...] are always marked by square brackets. Emphases in the text are those of the authors, or marked as "by me" - if different. Spelling has been modernized where appropriate. All translations into German are by me. Internet pages show the date of the most recent call. I highly recommend the purchase of the titles mentioned here.

[1] Krishnamurti, Jiddu: Einbruch in die Freiheit. Lotos 2006 p.23 ff

[2] Ibidem p. 85

[3] Steffanie Stahl: Jein! Bindungsängste erkennen und bewältigen. Ellert und Richter Verlag 2013 p. 52

[4] Ibidem p. 56

[5] Ibidem I p. 197

[6] Wardetzki, Bärbel: Eitle Liebe. Wie narzisstische Beziehungen scheitern oder gelingen können. Kösel 2012

[7] Ibidem p. 69 ff

[8] Ibidem p. 72 ff

[9] Townsend, John: Kto nam zatruwa zycie? (Original title: Who's pushing your buttons?) W drodze 2007 p.82

[10] Nay, W. Robert: Zwiazek bez gniewu. (Original title: Overcoming anger in your relationship.) Czarna Owca 2010 p. 79

[11] Nay p. 73

[12] Townsend p. 100

[13] Townsend p. 100

[14] Nay p. 120

[15] Nay p. 133

[16] Merkle, R./Wolf, D.: Gefühle verstehen, Probleme bewältigen. PAL 2007 P. 47

[17] Nay p. 203

[18] Nay p. 236

[19] Nay p. 235 ff

[20] Nay p. 243

[21] Steel p. 200

[22] Gajda, Monika and Marcin: Rozwoj. Jak wspolpracowac z laska? Pro Homine 2012 p. 91 ff

[23] Ibidem p. 106

[24] Hemfelt, Minirth, Meier: Mut zur Liebe. So gelingt ein Leben frei von Zwängen. GerthMedien 2007 p. 12

[25] Ibid p. 13

[26] Ibidem p. 14

[27] Satir, Virginia: Kommunikation-Selbstwert-Kongruenz. Junfermann 1994 p. 166

[28] Mut zur Liebe p. 57 ff

[29] Satir p. 151

[30] Mut zur Liebe p. 79

[31] Ibidem p. 83

[32] Ibidem p. 84

[33] Ibidem p. 84

[34] Ibid p 86 ff

[35] Ibidem p. 87

[36] Rettig, Daniel: https://www.alltagsforschung.de/schritt-fur-schritt-wie-kinder-gehen-lernen/ accessed 07/12/2019

[37] Stahl, Stefanie: Das Kind in dir muss Heimat finden. Der Schlüssel zur Lösung (fast) aller Probleme . Kailash 2015 p. 94

[38] Ibidem p. 96ff

[39] Green, Anselm https://www.tdh-online.de/archiv_2008_bis_2011/tdh_artikel_691.php accessed 08/05/2019

[40] Rozwoj p. 70

[41] Rozwoj p. 71 all translations by me

[42] Ibidem p. 88 ff

[43] Berking, Matthias: Training emotionaler Kompetenzen. Springer 2015 p. 19 ff [Italics highlighted by me].

[44] Ibidem p. 20 ff

[45] Ibidem p. 21 Emphasis by Berking

[46] Ibidem p. 21 ff

[47] Gefühle verstehen, Probleme bewältigen p. 167

[48] Krishnamurti p. 73

[49] Berking p. 25

[50] Rozwoj p. 127

[51] Gefühle verstehen, Probleme bewältigen p. 19

[52] Ibidem p. 20

[53] De Mello, Anthony: Der springende Punkt. Wach werden und glücklich sein. Herder 2011 p. 106 ff

[54] p Gefühle verstehen, Probleme bewältigen. 177

[55] Thurman, Chris: Lügen die wir glauben. Wie Sie Lebenslügen entlarven und befreit leben können. GerthMedien 2009 The book served as the basis and inspiration for this chapter.

[56] Bodenmann, G./Klinger, Ch.: Ohne Stress leben" Axel Springer 2013 p. 59 et seqq.

[57] Ibidem p. 98 ff

[58] Ibidem p. 61

[59] Bodenmann, Guy:. Bevor der Stress uns scheidet. Hogrefe 2016. p.95

[60] Stahl, Stefanie: "Das Kind in dir muss Heimat finden." S. 51

[61] Living without stress p. 204 ff

[62] Ibid p.76

[63] Ibidem p. 185

[64] Thurman p. 187

[65] Poletti,R./Dobbs, B: Akzeptieren, was ist. Loslassen und inneren Frieden finden. Scorpio 2015 p. 7

[66] Neff, Kristin: Selbstmitgefühl. Kailash 2012 p. 125

[67] Ibid. S. 204

[68] Byron, Katie: Lieben was ist. Wie vier Fragen Ihr Leben verändern können. Arcana 2002 p. 33

[69] Ibidem p. 35

[70] Ibidem p. 52 ff

[71] Ibidem p. 137

[72] Ibidem p. 105

[73] Ibidem p. 37

[74] Forward, Susan: Vergiftete Kindheit. Elterliche Macht und ihre Folgen. Goldmann 1993 p. 223 ff

[75] Dalai Lama: Die Weisheit des Verzeihens. Bastei Lübbe2008. S. 50

[76] Ricard, Matthieu: Glück. KnaurMenssana 2009 p. 225 ff.

[77] Ebenda p.54

[78] Welzer, Harald: Selbst denken. Eine Anleitung zum Widerstand. Fischer 2017 p.30

[79] https://de.wikipedia.org/wiki/Kognitive_Dissonanz accessed 07/13/2019

[80] Ricard p. 173

[81] Catalino, Lahnna I., Algoe, Sara B., and Fredrickson, Barbara L. https://www.ncbi.nlm.nih.gov/pmc/articles/PMC5533095/ accessed 07/13/2019

[82] Mut zur Liebe p. 148

[83] Krishnamurti p. 23

[84] Mut zur Liebe p. 161

[85] Rinpoche, Sogyal: Das tibetische Buch vom Leben und vom Sterben. KnaurMenssana 2013 p. 53

[86] Gefühle verstehen, Probleme bewältigen p. 137-138

[87] Ibidem p. 137

[88] Gottman, John M.: Die 7 Geheimnisse der glücklichen Ehe . Ullstein 2012 p. 308

[89] Tschechne, Rainer: Die Angst vor dem Glück. Warum wir uns selbst im Weg stehen. Herbig 2012 p. 83/ p. 161

[90] Cloud, Henry: Poszukiwana poszukiwany. (Original title: How to get a date worth keeping) W drodze 2010 p. 138 ff.

[91] Ibidem p. 148

[92] Santagati, Steve:. Mannual. So funktioniert der Mann. Fischer 2010 p. 285 ff

[93] Bodenmann p. 214

[94] Bodenmann p. 214

[95] Bodenmann p. 171

[96] Gottman p. 32

[97] Thiel, Christian: Liebe ist, den Partner nicht so zu nehmen wie er ist. Südwest 2016. p. 143 Emphasis mine.

[98] Retzer, Arnold: Lob der Vernunftehe. Fischer 2018 p. 171

[99] Ibidem p. 171

[100] Gottman p. 83

[101] Thiel p. 145

[102] Gottman p. 188/ 189

[103] Bittner, G. / Schwarz, E.: Emotion Selling. Messbar mehr verkaufen durch neue Erkenntnisse der Neurokommunikation. Gabler 2010 p. 177ff

[104] Rosenberg, Marshall B.: Gewaltfreie Kommunikation. Eine Sprache des Lebens. Junfermann 2013 p. 37

[105] Ibidem p. 99

[106] Emotion Selling. P. 16ff

[107] Ibid. P. 52 Emphasis mine.

[108] Gottman p. 179

[109] Ibidem p. 87

[110] Ibidem p. 105

[111] Ibidem p. 158

[112] Ibidem p. 25

[113] Ibidem p. 36

[114] Ibidem p. 112

[115] Ibidem p. 226

[116] Ibid. P. 39ff

[117] Ibid p, 214